FEW LIVING WR— [barcode] —to attract so mu— interest and enthu— troversy and adul— —on. Yet oddly enough (ou— —large amateur Tolkien clubs) no one has thoroughly explored the origins of Tolkien's work, "The Lord of the Rings," nor attempted to relate this modern masterpiece to the long history of magnificent epics of which it is both a part and a glorious example.

"A LOOK BEHIND THE LORD OF THE RINGS" is a knowledgable and enormously readable analysis of the history of epic, from the ancient Sumerian hero-sagas to the Greek myths to the Norse mythology and on down through *Beowulf* and the *Niebelungenleid* to the Siegfried and Brunhilde story: with, of course, particular reference to how "THE LORD OF THE RINGS" fits into this titanic tradition and where its root and sources lie. Lin Carter's book is fascinating reading for the millions of Ring-lovers, (for those who come to this book as Tolkien novices, there is a detailed synopsis of the trilogy) a most appropriately happy introduction to a world of wonder.

This is an original publication—not a reprint.

TOLKIEN:

A Look Behind
"The Lord of the Rings"

~~~~~~~~~~~~~~~~~~~~~~~~~~~~

Lin Carter

BALLANTINE BOOKS　●　NEW YORK

Author's Note

I am indebted to many persons for help, cooperation, and encouragement: their assistance has made this a better book than it might otherwise have been. I would like to express my gratitude to Mr. Ian Ballantine for his patience and interest in this project; to Mr. W. H. Auden for his advice, suggestions, and information; to my good friend and sometime collaborator, Mr. L. Sprague de Camp, for sharing with me his impressions of Professor Tolkien as he lives and works today, the results of a visit Mr. de Camp made to the Tolkien home in 1967; to Mr. Edmund R. Meskys, coeditor of *Niekas* and current Thain of the Tolkien Society of America, for his enthusiasm and encouragement in this project from its inception and for his generosity in providing me with a complete set of the Society's official organ, *The Tolkien Journal*; and to Mr. Rayner Unwin of George Allen and Unwin, Professor Tolkien's British publishers, for providing certain needed information. I am also grateful to many members of the Tolkien Society who have given help along the way and who, unfortunately, are too numerous to list.

I should also like to make it clear at this time that my book is by no means to be considered either an "official" or an "approved" study of *The Lord of the Rings*. Save for those places, clearly indicated in the text, where I am directly quoting the ideas or opinions of others, I am solely and completely responsible for the content of this book—including, of course, whatever errors of fact, emphasis, or interpretation it may contain. It is not to be assumed that anything in this book reflects the opinions of my publisher, Ballantine Books, or, for that matter, of Professor Tolkien himself.

LIN CARTER

Hollis, Long Island, New York

Contents

TOLKIEN:
A Look Behind
The Lord of the Rings

Orcs, and talking trees, and leagues of grass, and galloping riders, and glittering caves, and white towers and golden halls, and battles, and tall ships sailing.

J. R. R. TOLKIEN: *The Return of the King*

An Introduction

Only three or four books in a lifetime give us anything that is of real importance.

MARCEL PROUST, *Remembrance of Things Past*

~~~~~~

SUDDENLY it seems that nearly everyone is reading a very long and very peculiar book called *The Lord of the Rings*.

Science fiction fans were the first to discover it. They read and discussed it avidly in their small-circulation privately published amateur magazines called fanzines. No one even noticed or, if they did, probably did not think twice about it. As is well known, science fiction fans read that crazy rocketship stuff; if they can swallow that, they can take anything.

But before long, *The Lord of the Rings* was being talked about and argued over in Greenwich Village espresso houses, then in high-school yards and on college campuses. It was even explored and sometimes praised by literary folk like Anthony Boucher and W. H. Auden, Richard Hughes and C. S. Lewis. And, finally, it somehow got into the hands of the "general

1

reader," who usually subsists on fat novels from *The New York Times'* best-seller list.

The psychedelic-poster-and-button set (who came along after the book did) adopted *The Lord of the Rings* with little goat-cries of bliss. And today it is even mentioned at glossy East-side cocktail parties. In fact, *everyone* seems to have just completed it, has just begun it, or is just about to read it over for the second time.

Although *LOTR* (as its admirers acronymically refer to the trilogy, pronounced to rhyme with "boater") has been in print in this country for a full dozen years, interest in this odd and lengthy novel seems to grow steadily, rather than diminishing to eventually fade into that genteel literary limbo that claims 99 out of every 100 new fictions. Hardly a month passes without the flaws or merits of Professor Tolkien's three-decker novel being praised or condemned by an article in *Saturday Review* or *Seventeen, The New Yorker* or *Saturday Evening Post, Esquire* or *Holiday, The Nation* or *Triumph*.

Entrepreneurs, ever eager to clamber aboard the bandwagon of every new fad that goes whooping and jingling by, seized upon *LOTR* with loud hosannas. An astonishing variety of Tolkieniana is now on sale, from four-color travel posters with the headline "Come to Middle-earth!" to gorgeously decorated 25-inch-by-38-inch wallmaps of Tolkien's imaginary world that make the more mundane productions of Rand McNally look pallid by comparison. Along Greenwich Village's shop-lined streets you can purchase lapel buttons that claim "Frodo Lives!" or applaud "Go Go Gandalf"—appropriately rendered, of course, into Tolkien's invented language and runic alphabet, Elvish. Even so staid and literary a firm as Caedmon Records offers a disc whereon the good Professor may be heard reading some of the poems from *LOTR* in his own language! *

All across the country local clubs of Tolkien-infatuated readers, loosely confederated under the banners of The Tolkien Society of America, are springing up like mushrooms after the rainy season. Far-scattered Tolkienists have for some years past been keeping in touch with each other via the U.S. mails, issuing a number of mimeographed amateur magazines whose Tolkienish titles, such as *Entmoot* and *I Palantir* and *Green Dragon* and *The Tolkien Journal,* make no mystery of their principal topic of discussion.

While Tolkien's readers are unanimously in favor of his style of fiction, literary critics and reviewers on both sides of the Atlantic register a wide range of differing viewpoints. America's distinguished Edmund Wilson in *The Nation* for April 14, 1956, articulated the case for His Majesty's Loyal Opposition; sourly comparing Tolkien's prose to that of Howard Pyle, he scorned the verse with hearty contempt and summed up his case with the observation: "It is essentially a children's book—a children's book which has somehow got out of hand"; and I do not think he was entirely aiming this remark at the fact that the trilogy adds up to a hefty 1,300-odd pages of small type.

At the other end of the critical spectrum are the *New Statesman & Nation,* holding the opinion that "It is a story magnificently told, with every kind of colour, and movement, and greatness," and the New York

* The title is *Poems and Songs of Middle Earth,* Caedmon catalogue number TC 1231; the price is $5.95.

Herald Tribune, calling the work "An extraordinary, a distinguished piece of work"; Mr. Richard Hughes, discussing *LOTR* as a heroic romance conceived and written on a scale that has not been attempted for centuries, considers it impossible to praise by mere comparisons and ends helplessly: "What can I say then? For *width* of imagination it almost beggars parallel, and it is nearly as remarkable for its vividness and for the narrative skill which carries the reader on, enthralled, for page after page."

It is this amazing range of differing critical opinions, and the vigor and enthusiasm with which they are pressed, that make the book so controversial. Indeed, I suppose it could be said with considerable truth that here is *one* book on which it is almost impossible to remain neutral. You either read it with rapt, absorbed fascination—or you can hardly endure to read it at all and generally get bogged down in the first thirty pages.

The odd thing about these reviews is that there is a germ of truth in even the most negative of them. Mr. Wilson's remark about the trilogy's being "a children's book" is not unperceptive—nor is it unfair, although I dare say he meant the term in a derogatory sense. In the course of a full-page article on the third volume of the trilogy (in *The New York Times Book Review* for January 22, 1956), Pulitzer Prize-winning poet W. H. Auden praised the Professor for his handling of epic materials and went on to state that he "succeeded more completely than any previous writer in this genre in using the traditional properties of the Quest, the heroic journey, the Numinous Object," and so on, while at the same time "satisfying our sense of historical and social reality." He concludes with the opinion that, in one way at least, Tolkien "has succeeded where Milton failed."

The late Oxford professor, distinguished lay theologian C. S. Lewis (himself the author of several brilliant, thoughtful fantasy novels and a close personal friend of Tolkien, who heard much of *The Lord of the Rings* read aloud in manuscript), praised the trilogy and pointed out that "If Ariosto rivalled it in invention (in fact, he does not) he would still lack its heroic seriousness." Naomi Mitchinson also commented on this element, remarking that the work is to be taken quite as seriously as Malory; and Richard Hughes expressed the opinion that nothing had been attempted on such a scale since Spenser's *Faerie Queene*.

For a work of modern fiction seriously compared to Ariosto, Malory, and Spenser, *The Lord of the Rings* has proved an astonishingly popular commercial success. Sales of the hardcover edition moved slowly but steadily in this country for about nine years. It was not until the trilogy began appearing in paperback editions —the first from Ace Books in June 1965 and four months later Tolkien's own revision from Ballantine— that Tolkien began to make publishing history. For a 1,300-page trilogy to sell a quarter of a million copies in ten months is certainly extraordinary. As the author of eighteen moderately popular fantasy or science fiction books myself, I can assure you that to sell over 250,000 copies of a paperback set costing from $2.25 (Ace) to $2.85 (Ballantine) is an utterly astounding feat.

Exactly what is this enormously long and very unusual book? Here, as in critical estimates, opinions differ vastly. Is it, as Edmund Wilson suggests, just a super-king-sized children's book? A sort of fairytale for grown-ups, like the exquisite short stories Lord Dunsany used to write in his *Book of Wonder* and its sequels? But who ever heard of a 1,300-page fairy tale? Or is it a ponderous and old-fashioned allegory, like those of Dean Swift and Spenser—an allegory on the struggle of light against darkness, good against evil, or even on the ideological conflict between East and West?

If it is just a fantasy novel, an entertaining work of fiction, why did its author provide so extensive a critical apparatus, in the form of 134 pages of appendices, including maps, lists of kings, and genealogical charts, calendars, alphabets, and linguistic notes, and a historical outline of his imaginary Second and Third Ages of Middle Earth, covering 6,462 years?

Is it a genuine work of literature, a product of a certain form of imaginative genius, such as we have seldom seen since Sir Thomas Malory composed his *Morte d'Arthur?* Or is it just a tedious and cumbersome literary oddity, an eccentric Don's hobby?

This book hopes to answer these questions.

1.

The Lives And Times
of Professor Tolkien

> I have wandered in many lands, seeking
> the lost regions from which my birth
> into this world exiled me, and the
> company of creatures such as I myself.
> BERNARD SHAW

> L'homme n'est rien, l'oeuvre tout.
> GUSTAVE FLAUBERT

The author of *The Lord of the Rings* is J. R. R. Tolkien. The initials stand for John Ronald Reuel—the last
being a family name. As for Tolkien, it is a German
name (the Professor is of German descent, which may
partly explain his lifelong interest in what W. H.
Auden calls "the Northern thing"; but of this, more
later), and it is pronounced, variously, "Tul-KEEN" or
"TOL-kin."

Although both of his parents come from Birmingham, in northwestern Warwickshire, England, Tolkien
himself was born, on January 3, 1892, in Bloemfon-
tein, a city in the central portion of the Union of South
Africa. He was extremely young when his father, Arthur Reuel Tolkien, died. His mother brought the children (Tolkien has a brother) back to her native city,
and Tolkien was raised in Birmingham. He attended
the King Edward VI School in that city, one of En-

7

gland's largest provincial municipalities, with a population of well over one million.

Birmingham is a world center of manufacturing and industry, with steel production plants and factories belching sooty smoke over grimy streets lined with bleak rows of brick houses. I have sometimes wondered if the grim, dark city of his boyhood years did not in some part contribute to Tolkien's vision of Mordor, the evil land of darkness and terror in *The Lord of the Rings*, with harsh, cindery deserts and barren, sterile plains. But what is more certain is that the green fields and hills of the countryside which surrounded Birmingham in the late 1890's and early 1900's provided a framework for his vision of the Shire, that placid and pleasant land where the Hobbits of his imagination dwell. We have Tolkien's own word for such a connection. In an interview conducted on March 2, 1966, by transatlantic telephone between Henry Resnik (a writer preparing an article on Tolkien for the *Saturday Evening Post*) and the Professor, Tolkien was asked how he got "the Northern thing." He replied:

> Well, my parents both came from Birmingham in England. I happened to be born there [Bloemfontein] by accident. But it had this effect; my earliest memories are of Africa, but it was alien to me, and when I came home, therefore, I had for the countryside of England both the native feeling and the personal wonder of somebody who comes to it. I came to the English countryside when I was about 3½ or 4—it seemed to me wonderful. It you really want to know what Middle-earth is based on, it's my wonder and delight in the earth as it is, particularly the natural earth.*

---

* From a verbatim transcript of the Resnik-Tolkien interview as published in the amateur magazine *Niekas*, No. 18, dated "late Spring, 1967," and copyright 1967 by Niekas Publications.

In the article which Mr. Resnik made from this interview ("The Hobbit-Forming World of J. R. R. Tolkien," in the *Saturday Evening Post* for July 2, 1966), he summarized much of the above quotation and concludes the passage by noting: "He readily admits that the Shire of his trilogy has its roots in the English countryside" and that Tolkien shaped rural England, "one of the major interests of his life," to his own literary purposes.

Birmingham had been the home of Watt and Darwin. Hence it was not only one of the birthplaces of the Industrial Revolution, but also a center of scientific inquiry. The famous physicist Sir Oliver Lodge taught there. Sir William Herschel, the distinguished astronomer who discovered the planet Uranus, made Birmingham his home for some years as well.

But science and industry aside, Birmingham is not without a place in the history of the fine arts, for it was also the home of the noted Pre-Raphaelite artist, Sir Edward Burne-Jones, who created a magnificent stained-glass window for its cathedral church.

In 1904, when Tolkien was a boy of twelve, his mother died. From that point on he and his brother were raised by a Roman Catholic priest. Tolkien went from King Edward's school to Exeter College, Oxford, but before he could take his degree, the First World War interrupted. At the age of twenty-three Tolkien entered the Lancashire Fusiliers.

The following year, 1916, he married Miss Edith Bratt, who was later to become the mother of his three sons and one daughter.

Tolkien served with the Fusiliers from 1915 until 1918. With the collapse of Germany and the signing of the Armistice, he returned home and went back to his college. He received his M.A. (Oxon) in 1919.*

As a young man Tolkien became fascinated by languages to such an unusual degree that he diverted himself with the invention of new ones. After taking his degree, Tolkien worked for about two years as an assistant on the famous *Oxford English Dictionary* before beginning his career as a teacher. In 1920 he was a Reader in the English Language at the University of Leeds. His first major work of scholarship was published two years later: *A Middle-English Vocabulary* (1922). During the years 1924 and 1925 he was a Professor of the English Language at Leeds. During this time he published, with E. V. Gordon, his critical text of *Sir Gawain and the Green Knight,* the famous fourteenth-century poem by an unknown contemporary of Chaucer which Tolkien is, at the time of this writing (late 1968), translating into modern English verse.

In 1925 he left Leeds and came to Pembroke College at Oxford. For the next twenty years he remained there as Rawlinson and Bosforth Professor of Anglo-Saxon. By this time he found himself busily working out the sort of lands and countries in which his imaginary languages might be spoken, and before long he began making up stories about them. In 1926 Tolkien

---

* "Oxon" in parenthesis after a degree indicates that the degree was taken at one of the twenty-one colleges which make up the University of Oxford. To be precise, it stands for the term *Oxoniensis,* the Latin for "of Oxford." Beyond his Master of Arts degree, Tolkien has several honorary degrees, including Hon. D. Litt. from University College, Dublin. Since he has no Ph.D. degree, his proper title is "Professor," not "Doctor" Tolkien, as he is sometimes incorrectly termed. Tolkien is also entitled to the letters F.R.S.L., designating him as a Fellow of the Royal Society of Literature.

became a Fellow of Pembroke College. Many years later, he was to become an Emerson Fellow of Merton College and also an Honorary Fellow of Exeter College which, of course, was his alma mater.

His years at Pembroke were fruitful. While teaching Anglo-Saxon, he published "Chaucer as a Philologist" (1934) and, two years later, "Beowulf: the Monster and the Critics," two influential papers. By this time he had become a highly regarded English philologist. Philology which, according to the dictionary, is the study of written records, the establishment of their authenticity and of their original form, and the determination of their meaning, is a branch of linguistics, of course; considering the fascination languages hold for Tolkien, it is a natural field for his endeavors.

Following his study of *Beowulf* came something quite different. In 1937, when Tolkien was forty-five years old, he published a little book for children called *The Hobbit, or, There and Back Again*. And thereby hangs a tale.

For some years—as early as 1935, perhaps—he had found himself amusing his children by telling them tales of the imaginary world he had invented. This made-up world of Middle-earth, as he called it (borrowing the term from Norse mythology), and its languages and landscapes, its heroes and their histories, had come to occupy his attention more and more. It was at the urging of some of his colleagues at Oxford that he first began writing a children's book based on the stuff of these tales.

In doing this, Tolkien was of course following in the hallowed footsteps of another Oxford Don, a lecturer in mathematics at Christ Church, Oxford, who died when Tolkien was six years old. This Don—a gawky, shy, stuttering fellow, with the cumbersome name of Dodgson—earned his place in the history of letters when he extemporized a story to entertain three children of a friend during a hot afternoon as they poled up the river to Godstow. The precise date was July 4, 1862 —surely the second most momentous Fourth of July in human history, for the impromptu fairystory, later written down and expanded and presented to one of the children, became known to millions of children the world over as *Alice's Adventures in Wonderland.*

The immortal *Alice* is far from being the only famous children's classic that took its shape while being told aloud to children. Over the Christmas season in 1901, when Tolkien was nine years old, a certain Scots playwright named Barrie took his neighbors, the Davies boys, to see a mediocre play for children. While seated in the theater, it occurred to him that he could make as good a play as this out of the fairystories he had been making up to amuse his young friends—and *Peter Pan* was conceived.

Similarly, on a May evening in 1904, when Tolkien was twelve, a frightfully respectable Secretary of the Bank of England, who had for some time been making up bedtime stories for the entertainment of his little son Alastair (called "Mouse"), found he had suddenly introduced a certain intrepid Toad into these tales. Later, when Mouse was away from home on vacation, the tales had to be continued in the form of long illustrated letters; and the first words of what would someday be known as *The Wind in the Willows* were set down on paper.

And somewhat earlier, across the ocean in Chicago, a gentleman from Syracuse, New York, forty-four years old and with four small sons to support, delighted the children by telling them tales of magical adventures he made up. As a businessman, Mr. Baum was not very successful. He had tried his hand at an amazing variety of enterprises, from writing Irish musical comedies to running a variety store and publishing a newspaper. He had also, rather surprisingly, written some nine books, including one on the fine art of decorating shop windows and another (his first), a brief treatise of only seventy-one pages, upon the mating, rearing, and management of chickens.

His tenth book was to be something quite different: *The Wonderful Wizard of Oz.*

The book which eventually took shape as *The Hobbit* was published when Tolkien was forty-five. C. S. Lewis, also teaching at Oxford in those days, persuaded Tolkien to submit the manuscript to a publisher. The London house of George Allen and Unwin, Ltd., accepted the book. It was not unsuccessful.

The New Statesman & Nation observed: "His wholly original story of adventure among goblins, elves and dragons . . . gives . . . the impression of a well-informed glimpse into the life of a wide other-world; a world wholly real, and with a quite matter-of-fact, supernatural natural-history of its own"; the article further remarked that it was a triumph of the book that the new genus Hobbit rings as true as do the time-honored genera of goblin, troll, or elf.

The Times of London called it "A fascinating excursion into the early English scene" and commended the work as "a solidly delightful book." *The Observer* waxed a bit more enthusiastic: "Professor Tolkien's finely written saga of dwarves and elves, fearsome goblins and trolls, in a spacious country of far-off and long ago . . . a full-length tale of traditional magic beings . . . an exciting epic of travel, magical adventure . . . working up to a devastating climax."

The success of *The Hobbit* in its native England has been more than equaled on this side of the ocean. The Houghton Mifflin Company of Boston brought out the American edition, which promptly won the *Herald Tribune* prize as the best children's book of the year. Since then it has continued in print, through thirty years and many many printings, to become one of the best-loved of recent children's classics, easily on a level with *Mary Poppins* and *Doctor Dolittle* and *The Borrowers.*

Unlike that greatest and most popular of all American fairytales, *The Wizard of Oz,* which was, for the first half-century or so of its history, persistently and universally ignored and unmentioned by the critics, historians, and reviewers of children's books and slighted by librarians and teachers (nobody loved Oz but the several million children who have taken it to their hearts), Tolkien's *Hobbit* is regularly listed on the "approved reading" roster as one of the most notable and highly recommended of perennial children's classics. And it has been an incredible publishing success: in the Ballantine paperback edition alone, as of October, 1967, *The Hobbit* has sold an unbelievable total of well over one million copies.

After *The Hobbit,* Tolkien produced in 1938 a critical essay, "On Fairy-Stories," first delivered as an Andrew Lang Lecture at the University of St. Andrews (it was reprinted in 1965 as part of *Tree and Leaf*). Other scholarly papers followed, and in 1945 Tolkien left Pembroke to take a post at Oxford as Merton Professor of the English Language and Literature. In that position he remained until he retired in 1959. Between 1937, when *The Hobbit* was published, and 1954 the only two pieces of fiction the Professor published were a slight tale called "Leaf by Niggle" (which appeared in the *Dublin Review* during 1947) and a slim but completely delicious novelette-length fairystory called "Farmer Giles of Ham," which came out in Great Britain in 1949 and had its American edition from Houghton Mifflin in the following year. All these works have subsequently been reprinted by Ballantine Books in *The Tolkien Reader*.

But the writing of *The Hobbit* had not exhausted the Professor's interest in Middle-earth—far from it. "Soon after *The Hobbit* was written and before its publication in 1937" (I am quoting from Professor Tolkien's Foreword to the Ballantine Books edition of *LOTR*) he was at work on another tale of his imaginary world—a more serious and adult story this time, and painted upon a more vast and mighty canvas—a new book whose composition was to largely occupy him for the next full thirteen years of his life.

He was writing *The Lord of the Rings*.

2.

How *The Lord of the Rings* Came to Be Written

Faerie contains many things besides elves and fays, and besides dwarfs, witches, trolls, giants, or dragons: it holds the seas, the sun, the moon, the sky, and the earth, and all things that are in it: tree and bird, water and stone, wine and bread, and our-selves, mortal men.

J. R. R. TOLKIEN, *On Fairy-Stories*

Tolkien's friends among his Oxford colleagues centered about C. S. Lewis and made up a circle, which included W. H. Lewis (his brother); the writer Charles Williams, whose several fine novels on occult and mystical subjects are (I feel, unfortunately) better known to American readers than his two fascinating volumes of Arthurian verse; and a number of other congenial souls, including John Wain, Roy Campbell, and David Cecil. They made up an informal group, calling themselves the Inklings, and gathered in C. S. Lewis' rooms at Magdalen College every Thursday evening after dinner.

It was this fortunate group who were the first to hear of *The Lord of the Rings* (or Tolkien's new Hobbit, as they called it). In fact, not only did they hear *of* it, but they heard the actual work itself read aloud by its author page by page. For it was the happy habit of

16

the Inklings, when the stream of conversation had run dry, to read to each other from works in progress. (This stream of conversation, by the way, wandered lazily through a haphazard forest of likely and unlikely subjects—"from beer to *Beowulf,* to torture, Tertullian, bores, the contractual theory of medieval kingship, and odd place-names," as W. H. Lewis recalled it in an introduction to his edition of the *Letters of C. S. Lewis,* published by Harcourt, Brace in 1966.)

Professor Tolkien began writing *The Lord of the Rings* when he was forty-four; and "the composition . . . went on at intervals during the years 1936 to 1949," according to his Foreword to the Ballantine edition of the trilogy. In the light of the world fame that eventually came to *LOTR,* it is amusing to "overhear," as it were, casual references to it in C. S. Lewis' letters from this thirteen-year period. Witness this passing mention, typical of many such, which Lewis made in a note to his brother dated November 11, 1939:

On Thursday we had a meeting of the Inklings—you and Coghill both absent unfortunately. We dined at the Eastgate. I have never in my life seen Dyson so exuberant— "A roaring cataract of nonsense." The bill of fare afterwards consisted of a section of the new Hobbit book from Tolkien, a nativity play from Ch. Williams (unusually intelligible for him, and approved by all), and a chapter out of the book on the Problem of Pain from me.

Or this, from another letter written to W. H. Lewis and dated December 3 of the same year:

The usual Thursday party did not meet . . . so I went up to Tolkien's. We had a very pleasant evening drinking gin and lime-juice and reading our recent chapters to each other—his from the new Hobbit.

17

The Lord of the Rings is an extremely long work of fiction: at a very conservative estimate, the trilogy works out to something over five hundred thousand words—*half a million* words. Thus it is little wonder that Tolkien took some thirteen years to write it.

During a large portion of this time the Inklings heard the book read aloud: I do not know whether Tolkien read the entire trilogy to them, but the chances that he did are quite good. C. S. Lewis first refers to it in his *Letters* in 1939; W. H. Lewis, in his introductory memoir to the *Letters,* recalls hearing Tolkien read a chapter of *LOTR* "at most of the meetings" throughout 1946; the Inklings therefore listened to it through at least eight years.

Though they no doubt discussed it and commented upon it, they did not, apparently, have any appreciable influence on the trilogy as it took shape. Everyone concerned seems quite adamant on this point. Four years after the final volume of the trilogy had been published, C. S. Lewis commented on the subject in a letter of May 15, 1959, written in reply to a query from Charles Moorman about inter-influences among the Inklings.

Charles Williams certainly influenced me and I perhaps influenced him. But after that I think you would draw a blank. No one ever influenced Tolkien—you might as well try to influence a bandersnatch. We listened to his work, but could affect it only by encouragement. He has only two reactions to criticism: either he begins the whole work over again from the beginning or else takes no notice at all.

But Professor Tolkien had some slight influence, it would seem, on the author of *Perelandra, Out of the Silent Planet,* and *That Hideous Strength.* In another letter to Mr. Moorman (who had this time written to inquire concerning the origin of some of the more obscure mythic elements in *That Hideous Strength*), dated October 2, 1952, Lewis wrote: "Numinor is a mis-spelling of Numenor which, like the 'true West,' is a fragment from a vast private mythology invented by Professor J. R. R. Tolkien. At the time we all hoped that a good deal of that mythology would soon become public through a romance which the Professor was then contemplating. Since then the hope has receded." Since this was written two years before the first volume of *The Lord of the Rings* was published, the implication is that towards the end Tolkien temporarily abandoned the work.

When Henry Resnik interviewed Tolkien and mentioned an opinion he had heard that Charles Williams and George Macdonald* had "a very deep influence"

---

* George Macdonald (1824–1905) was a Scots clergyman and close friend of Lewis Carroll. He wrote some of the first (and best) fantasies written for children in English, most importantly *At The Back of the North Wind* (1871) and *The Princess and the Goblin*. Chances are, however, that the books to which Mr. Resnik was referring were not these children's books but Macdonald's two brilliant fantasy-allegories written for adult readers: *Lilith* and *Phantastes*. I feel that Tolkien was quite honest in his denial of Macdonald's influence, for I can myself see no slightest trace of either of the above books on the trilogy. They did, however, have a very considerable hand in the shaping of C. S. Lewis' Perelandra trilogy, as did David Lindsay's remarkable novel, *A Voyage to Arcturus* (1920).

And since I have brought C. S. Lewis into the picture again, let me add that the third volume of the Perelandra trilogy—*That Hideous Strength*—which mentions Tolkien's Numenor and "the true West," was published in 1946, when the Professor was only three years away from the conclusion of his own trilogy. *Strength* was not, as might be expected, dedicated to Tolkien. For that honor, Lewis reserved what in my opinion are the most profound, and perhaps the most lasting, of all his fictions, *The Screwtape Letters*. There is no evidence that Tolkien ever dedicated anything to Lewis, although *LOTR* as a whole was originally dedicated in part to the Inklings, of whom Lewis was perhaps the central member.

on *The Lord of the Rings*, the Professor had this to say:

> Well, that's quite wrong. Williams had no influence on me at all. I didn't even know him very well. I'll tell you one thing on that point, one of the things I remember Lewis' saying to me—of course, Lewis was very influenced as you may know—was, "Confound you, nobody can influence you anyhow. I have tried but it's no good."

And as for Macdonald, Tolkien remarked in the same interview that "I now find that I can't stand George Macdonald's books at any price at all."

The only influence Tolkien will admit to these days (not counting, of course, the Northern mythology, which will be examined in detail in a subsequent chapter) is H. Rider Haggard's *She*.

The first volume of the trilogy is called *The Fellowship of the Ring*. George Allen and Unwin published the British edition in 1954, when Tolkien was sixty-two, only a few years from retirement. The dedication mentions the Inklings, "because they have already listened to it with a patience, and indeed with an interest, that almost leads me to suspect that they have Hobbit-blood in their venerable ancestry."

The second volume, *The Two Towers*, was also published that same year. The final portion, *The Return of the King*, came in 1955. The press reviews were in general laudatory. The *Guardian* called Tolkien a "born story-teller"; the *New Statesman & Nation* wrote: "It is a story magnificently told, with every kind of colour, and movement, and greatness." *Time and Tide*, in a review by C. S. Lewis, effused: "Here are beauties which pierce like swords or burn like cold iron; here is a book that will break your heart . . . good beyond hope."

But beyond the enthusiasm of the reviews, I seem to detect a certain bewilderment. Mr. Lewis compared the work to the mighty Italian romancer, Ludovico Ariosto, author of the *Orlando Furioso;* Miss Mitchison observed: "it's really super science fiction," but "one takes it as seriously as Malory." Other writers compared the book to Spenser, to Milton, to Dante, to the Brothers Grimm, and the like. Out of all this, I am left with the impression that, while the virtues and merits of the trilogy were more or less obvious, the sheer overwhelming complexity of the books left readers somewhat puzzled as to exactly what its genre was: allegory, satire, giant-sized fairytale, epic, romance, fantastic novel, or "super science fiction." The one point on which almost everyone agreed was that scarcely anything on this scale or in this form had been attempted since Edmund Spenser's *Faerie Queene.* (Spenser, an Elizabethan poet of Shakespeare's time, published the first portions of his 35,000-line romance in 1590.) The implication is that no one in the last three and a half centuries has attempted to write fantasy on the epic scale but for Tolkien. But in Chapter 13 it will become clear that this is not so.

The Lord of the Rings was not a tremendous success in Great Britain. In 1956, one year after the last volume appeared in England, Houghton Mifflin imported unbound copies to America. Although widely reviewed by major literary figures the trilogy did not command much attention. It was not until nine years later, when the paperback editions went into print, that Tolkien's work came to the attention of the millions who were to adopt it with such fantastic enthusiasm.

This is explained to some degree by the difference in price between the hardcover editions and the paperback printings. There was, in fact, a devoted group of admirers who owned the hardcover editions. However, relatively few persons will plunk down a cold fifteen dollars for a forbiddingly massive trilogy in small print. But when the same book is available for less than a dollar per volume and appears on every paperback stand and when, indeed, two competitive editions appear to the accompaniment of a great deal of publicity, then that book has a much better chance of coming to the attention of those who are prepared to enjoy it. Such, at any rate, was the case with *LOTR*.

In virtually no time at all, the trilogy in paperback was outselling everything else in campus bookshops all across the nation, topping even such hits on the Ivy League best-seller list as the perennial favorite, J. D. Salinger's *The Catcher in the Rye,* and *Lord of the Flies.* The trilogy, it seems, had at last found an immense audience that had been waiting for it all their lives. People did not just read it, they read and reread it over and over again. "Five times is not an uncommon record," wrote Henry Resnik. He went on to mention one reader who lost count after thirty complete readings.

In 1959, three years after the American paperback editions were printed, Professor Tolkien retired from Oxford to live quietly with his wife in a cottage in Headington. The retiring age at Oxford is sixty-six, and he had now reached that point in life. He remains a Fellow of his college in honor of his achievements, and his proper title today is Professor Emeritus.

He is still at work writing both his own original works and an occasional scholarly treatise or translation, but the teaching career that has occupied some thirty-five years of his life has come to a close.

3.

Tolkien Today

> Both of ancient times and our own; books, arms,
> And of men of unusual genius,
> Both of ancient times and our own,
>   in short the usual subjects
> Of conversation between intelligent men.
>
> EZRA POUND, *Canto XI*

Since completing *The Lord of the Rings,* Professor
Tolkien has lived quietly in a small, modest house, one
of a row of similar suburban homes, near Oxford.
More recently, owing in part to the distractions created
by the fame of *LOTR,* the professor has moved to a
home that provides a little more privacy. His children
are grown up and busy with their own lives and ca-
reers (his son, Christopher Tolkien, has followed in
the Professor's footsteps and is now a Lecturer in Old
English at New College, Oxford*). Professor and Mrs.
Tolkien live alone.

---

* Christopher Tolkien published in 1960 a scholarly work which
would be of considerable interest to his father's fans: an English
translation of *The Saga of King Heidrek the Wise,* in the series
called Nelson's Icelandic Texts. This Icelandic medieval romance
contains, rather amusingly, references to a number of characters
and places which occur in *The Lord of the Rings:* in particular, the
dwarves Durin and Dvalin, as well as the forest of Mirkwood.

The original house near Oxford to which Professor Tolkien retired was small and cluttered, filled with stacks of books. The Professor did his writing in the garage, which he had converted into a rude but serviceable study.

My friend, the American fantasy and science fiction writer L. Sprague de Camp, visited the Tolkiens a short time ago. He reports to me that the Professor, now seventy-six years old, is hale and hearty, as alert and keen-witted as ever. He is a little above average height, although heavy-set and stooped. He has thinning gray hair and cool, thoughtful, measuring eyes of gray. He speaks in a pleasant baritone voice, sometimes smokes a pipe, and (says de Camp) "is one of those people who has literally read everything, and can converse intelligently on just about any subject."

Far from living apart from the world, busied with the worlds of his own imagination, Tolkien takes a strong interest in what is going on, not only in the University and in England, but in world affairs as well. He reads a newspaper every day—in fact, he takes three. He is still an expert in his special field and still produces an occasional article on it. He has recently been working on new translations of *Sir Gawain and the Green Knight* and another medieval poem, *The Pearl.* These may well be in print before this book is published.

Since *LOTR,* however, he has published very little. In 1962 there was a slim collection of verse, in part reprinted from *LOTR* and in part new, titled *The Adventures of Tom Bombadil. Tree and Leaf,* made up of one fairytale, "Leaf by Niggle," and the essay "On Fairy-Stories," was published in 1965. For the Early English Text Society Tolkien edited an edition of *The*

Ancrene Wisse. This work—the title means something like "Guide for Anchoresses"—is a manual of spiritual discipline for the directresses of medieval religious communities; it is directly within Tolkien's special field, i.e. the literary and linguistic tradition of the English West Midlands.

There has also been a slim little tale, *Smith of Wooton Major* and a handsome volume called *The Road Goes Ever On*, a song cycle with words by Professor Tolkien and music by Donald Swann. Besides these, Tolkien had recently added some new material and a Foreword to the Ballantine edition of *LOTR*.

Beyond this, most of this time has been spent puttering with the very long-awaited sequel to *The Lord of the Rings*, which has been in the works during the past ten years. I refer to *The Silmarillion*.

This sequel—or, rather, *prequel*, if I may employ a useful neologism coined by the science fiction fan community (relevant here because the book takes place at an earlier age than *LOTR*) is reportedly close to completion. Early rumors had much to say about the prequel to *The Lord of the Rings*—mostly pure hearsay, based on wishful speculation or inference. It was going to be another triple-decker novel like the *Ring*. No—it would more probably be an encyclopedialike volume of notes, comparable to the appendices of chronologies, lists of kings, and so on, which conclude the third volume of the original trilogy. Speculation, as the saying goes, was rife.

It is now believed that *The Silmarillion* will be an actual narrative—"like *Paradise Lost*," says a Tolkien enthusiast named Hal Lynch of New York, reporting at a meeting of The Tolkien Society of America. (Mr. Lynch does not name the source from which he derives this authoritative statement. The meeting was in January, 1967.)

What is not so widely known is that Tolkien seems to have actually written *The Silmarillion* years before even *The Hobbit*. This came out of the invaluable Resnik-Tolkien interview published in *Niekas,* from which I quoted earlier. Tolkien told Resnik he wrote *The Silmarillion* first, but the publishers rejected it. Now that his later books have proved so successful, they are only too anxious to get on with publication.

The hold-up stems from two facts. First of all, of course, in the writing of *The Lord of the Rings,* Tolkien diverged in many places from the factual structure of information he originally put in the prequel. "And of course now it has to be made to fit *The Lord of the Rings,*" Tolkien told Mr. Resnik. The other delaying factor in Tolkien's age. "I'm an old man now, and I've got a short working day," he says. "I cannot go on working until two, as I used to."

Everyone is enormously interested in the appearance of *The Silmarillion.* One gentleman, Mr. Clyde S. Kilby, a Professor of English at Wheaton College, Illinois, went so far as to journey to England during the summer of 1966 and stayed with the Tolkiens to assist in the work involved in preparing the manuscript. Rumors are stirring concerning the precise shape and substance of the book (or books—one rumor has it that *The Silmarillion* will appear in four volumes). One young man, who actually claims to have read the work in manuscript, reports that it deals with the period from the first rebellion of Morgoth to the foundation of Gondor. According to Appendix B, the founding of Gondor took place in 3320 of the Second Age. It does not seem likely to me that the book would end at such an ambiguous point. I suspect the story continues for another 121 years, concluding in 3441, when Elendil and Gil-galad overthrow Sauron and are themselves destroyed, whereupon Isildur takes the Ring and the Second Age closes. This would be a more logical ending place for the story. But we shall have to wait and see. In any case, for those who have yet to read the trilogy, this discussion is without meaning or significance.

One further note, however. The title, *The Silmarillion,* refers to the history of mystic gems of strange power which were wrested from the Iron Crown of Morgoth in the First Age of Middle-earth. (*Silmaril* is the singular; the plural is *silmarilli.*) In his Appendix A to the trilogy Professor Tolkien states that there were only three unions of the High Elves and Men in marriage. The first of these was in the First Age, when the Elf princess Luthien Tinuviel, daughter of King Thingol Greycloak of Doriath and a woman of the Valar, wed Beren the son of Barahir, a mortal man of the Edain. Luthien and Beren together took a *silmaril* from the Iron Crown; it passed to their daughter, Elwing, who wed Eärendil the Mariner. Eärendil, with the power of the *silmaril* at his command, passed beyond the Shadows and came to "the Uttermost West" as the ambassador of both Elves and Men to plead for aid against Morgoth. He was not permitted to return to the mortal lands, but he and his ship were set in the skies as a star, a sign of hope to the dwellers in Middle-earth. There were two other *silmarilli* in the Crown. In Appendix A, I(i) the Professor lists both of the other *silmarilli* as lost at the end of the First Age, as "is told in *The Silmarillion,*" he adds. This may indicate that *The Silmarillion* (which I infer, from the title, to be

28

the story of the history of these three gems) is laid in the First, and not the Second, Age.

And so we have Professor Tolkien as he is today. At seventy-six he is still hale and hearty, living alone with his wife in a quiet suburb in retirement, his children grown up and moved away—the eldest is now fifty, the youngest is thirty-eight. He is an outspoken, even argumentative old gentleman, who enjoys his pipe, an occasional hike in the country, and a chat with a friend over a companionable bottle of beer.

He finds the attentions of his enthusiastic following rather embarrassing and his notoriety a bit of a bore. He particularly feels that studies of his work (such, I presume, as this one) to be an annoyance.* He feels they are premature. When asked if he approved of this sort of intensive research, he replied: "I do not, while I am alive anyhow." He went on to say that he has read some of these studies, "and they are very bad, most of them; they are nearly all either psychological analyses or they try to go into sources, and I think most of them rather vain efforts." (I am quoting from the Resnik-Tolkien interview in *Niekas*.)

I can well imagine how embarrassing it must be to a scholar of his distinction to realize that on college campus and in espresso shop he is a popular celebrity, almost a folk-hero like Bobby Dylan—not for his professorial career or scholarly works, but for his imaginative fiction.

Now, perhaps, it is time to take a good close look at

---

* Henry Resnik notes: "There are at least two men presently working on doctoral theses [on *LOTR*] at universities, and I have myself read a master's thesis on *The Lord of the Rings*."

his fiction. I intend to summarize *The Hobbit* and each of the three volumes of *The Lord of The Rings,* so that those who have not yet dipped into their pages will be able to get a rough idea of just what they are all about, in plot and theme and character, in order to follow the critical dissection of the trilogy in the second half of this book.

I hope it is clearly understood that in summarizing the more than 1,300 pages of the trilogy into a brief outline, many minor characters and incidents will of necessity have to go without mention. The discussion must be confined to the basic outline, the major elements; but for the fuller story I commend a reading of *The Lord of the Rings* itself. This capsule outline is no substitute for the genuine article, nor is it intended to be.

4.

Of Middle-Earth and the Story of *The Hobbit*

Come with me, ladies and gentlemen
who are in any wise weary of London:
come with me: and those that tire at all
of the worlds we know:
for we have new worlds here.
LORD DUNSANY, Preface to *The Book of Wonder*

~~~~~~~~~~~~~~~~~

Middle-earth, the scene of *The Hobbit* and *The Lord of the Rings,* is our own world at some unthinkably remote age before history—before even those prehistoric epics whose deeds and events are half-remembered in mythology.

Professor Tolkien tells us that the Shire and the other western lands that lie about it represent northwestern Europe, but he does not mean us to take this statement too seriously. The trilogy must not be thought to present a theoretical picture of some forgotten age of post-Atlantean history or any such claptrap —that we leave to the occultists.

Tolkien is merely telling a tale, and for no more serious purpose than the pure enjoyment in the tale. Although it is possible to trace many of his story themes and plot devices to their origins in northern mythology and literature, he certainly does not intend to hint that his readers should superimpose a map of ancient Europe and the Near East over his imaginary chart of Middle-earth, as one is supposed to do, for example, with the world of the Hyborian Age wherein the fantasy writer Robert E. Howard laid the scene for his swashbuckling stories of Conan the Cimmerian.*

As Tolkien bluntly put it, in reply to a direct question as to what he meant by Middle-earth: "It's only an old-fashioned word for 'world.' That's all. Look in the dictionary. It isn't another planet." And he is quite correct—it is, in fact, listed as an obsolete term for "the world" in Webster's Universal Unabridged Dictionary, Volume II, 1936 edition.

Tolkien uses the term more or less to represent "the lands of men," in the sense the Norse myths use the word *Midgard*. But *Midgard* does not mean "Middle-earth." Webster's tells us that *Midgard* (from the Icelandic *midhgardhr*) means literally "mid-yard," i.e. the middle ground between heaven and hell, where human beings dwell. Professor Tolkien did not have to look very far to find the term "Middle-earth." It abounds in many works of early English literature—such as the long poem called *The Alliterative Morte Arthur*, which was written down around 1360. The phrase also appears in the thirteenth-century ballad of *Thomas the Rhymer:*

---

* In the Conan stories—which, by the way, Tolkien has read and has said he rather enjoys—the land of "Stygia" is meant to be identified with a prehistoric version of Egypt, "Vendhya" with India, "Asgard" with the Scandinavian peninsula, "Hyrkania" with Russia, and so on. These Conan stories, originally written for the American pulp magazine *Weird Tales,* are pulp fiction at its most lurid and gory—and at its most colorful and sheerly entertaining.

> She said, "Thomas, take now leave of sun and moon,
>   And of the leaf that grows on tree;
> This twelvemonth must thou with me go,
>   And middle-earth shalt thou not see."

Tolkien's picture of Middle-earth during the Third Age is not very different from Europe during the Middle Ages. It is mostly made up of great and ancient forests, where dark things lurk, with here and there a patch of homely life—small farms and furrowed fields and little towns—forming islands of quiet, rural society amid the blackness of the wilderness. It is a world rising into the full noon of civilization, gradually exploring its limits and taming its wild places, half-remembering the high and noble civilizations of distant ages from whence it sprang—lost Númenor amidst the Sea, proud Arnor to the north and Gondor in the southern lands.

But it is a medieval world with this difference: like Greece in the mythological age before history began, men still share their world with beings that are not men, as the characters in Greek myth move through landscapes still inhabited by dryads and nymphs, tritons, fauns, satyrs, centaurs, and unearthly hybrid monsters.

In Middle-earth Men share the world (to which they are still comparative newcomers, whose ancestors came over-Sea out of the Uttermost West) with Dwarves, for example: rugged little people, gruff, hardy, and stubborn, who go clad in hooded cloaks and have long shaggy beards and bandy legs; who prefer the mines and caverns of their subterranean halls to the light of the upper world (much like old Ruggedo and his subjects in the Gnome Kingdom which lies across the Deadly Desert in the Oz books). They share it, too, with Elves—not the dainty, diminutive sprites of Elizabethan fancy, sleeping in buttercups and bathing in dewdrops, but bright, immortal beings of unearthly cold beauty and wisdom and purity, whose memories go back to the Elder Days before Good or Evil had yet come into Middle-earth. And there are the Ents, possibly the longest-lived of all, the weird but kindly "shepherds-of-trees," who are old as the mountains. And the Hobbits, of course: a humble, burrow-dwelling, sociable little folk who live close to the earth and everyday things, good gardeners, fond of tobacco and fireworks, birthday parties and genealogies, and quite uninterested in high heroic deeds, magic powers, and fantastic wars. There are also all manner of ugly and fearsome creatures, Dragons and Trolls and the Orcs (who are Goblins) and yet other bestial and ferocious beings and monsters.

The Hobbits, who play a central role in both *The Hobbit* and in the trilogy itself, are Professor Tolkien's own invention (as are the Ents, who bear little resemblance to any of the stock races of mythology, unlike the Dwarves, Elves, and Trolls, who were borrowed from Northern myth). They have lived for ages in a comfortable, fertile, sheltered land of their own, with very little intercourse with neighboring races. *The Hobbit* and *LOTR* (whose pretended source is an imaginary Hobbit chronicle called The Red Book of Westmarch) form the story of how a few hobbits emerge from the seclusion of their sunny little land and play a role of vast importance in the mighty events that shape the history of this Third Age. Not of themselves adventurous, they have the role forced upon them by changing times, for the secluded safety of their land, the Shire, has been breeched.

The world has fallen on dark times. In an earlier age, the Dúnedain, the mighty Kings of Men, had come to this land out of Númenor over the Sea and built great kingdoms. The Elves were their teachers and shared with them their ancient wisdom and lore, and it was a bright and golden time. But now the Elves have begun to withdraw from Middle-earth, the proud kings of Gondor have vanished into the dim mists of legend, and a Dark Power is growing in the East. Already—even in *The Hobbit,* which serves as a sort of prologue to the trilogy—you can detect the gathering of the Dark Power. That mighty forest that was called of old Greenwood the Great has fallen under a malign influence and now goes under the grim name of Mirkwood, and its ways are no longer wholesome to the unwary wanderer. Orcs and Trolls are seen in unwonted numbers, boldly appearing in places where they were rarely glimpsed before, and wild Wargs (as the evil wolves beyond the edge of the Wild are called) are afield.

This is the setting for the beginning of Tolkien's story.

THE HOBBIT

Of all these races, the Hobbits are Tolkien's own favorite invention, and they play a major part in his vast epic. In the opening pages of *The Hobbit* he describes them as:

They are (or were) little people, about half our height,

and smaller than the bearded Dwarves. Hobbits have no beards. There is little or no magic about them, except the ordinary everyday sort which helps them to disappear quietly and quickly when large stupid folk like you and me come blundering along. . . . They are inclined to be fat in the stomach; they dress in bright colours (chiefly green and yellow); wear no shoes, because their feet grow natural leathery soles and thick warm brown hair like the stuff on their heads (which is curly); have long clever brown fingers, good-natured faces, and laugh deep fruity laughs (especially after dinner, which they have twice a day when they can get it).

Mr. Bilbo Baggins of Bag End in the Shire is a typical Hobbit. A respectable bachelor of some means, he lives alone in his *smial,* perfectly content with things just as they are. A *smial* is a burrow, a "Hobbit-hole" in the side of a hill, with a round front door whose knob is exactly in the center and which opens on a tube-shaped tunnel with paneled walls and floors tiled and carpeted, with many little tunnel rooms branching off from it on the same level (no going up or down stairs for Hobbits) which were used for bedrooms, cellars, pantries, wardrobes, kitchens, and the like.

Mr. Baggins is smoking his pipe on the front step when he is accosted by a stranger—a wandering Wizard named Gandalf, who is searching for someone to join him in an adventure. Gandalf, as he first appears in these pages, is anything but prepossessing; he is "a little old man with a tall pointed blue hat, a long grey cloak, a silver scarf over which his long white beard hung down below his waist, and immense black boots," leaning on his staff. Bilbo tries to make it plain that he is certainly not interested in leaving his warm and comfy Hobbit-hole for unpleasant adventures in the wild world beyond the Shire. In order to get rid of the bothersome old fellow without being rude, he hastily invites him to tea the next day.

When teatime comes, Bilbo answers the door and finds on his doorstep, instead of the old magician, a Dwarf named Dwalin with a long blue beard tucked into his golden belt. Then, in rapid succession, there arrive a very old-looking Dwarf named Balin son of Fundin, with a white beard and a scarlet hood, then two Dwarves named Kíli and Fíli with blue hoods, silver belts and yellow beards, and then a whole pile of others—Dori, Nori, Ori, Óin and Glóin, Bifur, Bofur, Bombur, and the great Thorin Oakenshield himself, the son of Thráin the son of Thrór, who of old was King under the Mountain—thirteen dwarves in all, with a grinning Gandalf at the end of the line.

Flustered, Bilbo tries to make the best of a bad situation and offers them his hospitality. The Dwarves feast from his larder, and after tea they take out their musical instruments and fill the Hobbit-hole with a haunting wild song:

> Far over the misty mountains cold
> To dungeons deep and caverns old
> We must away ere break of day
> To seek the pale enchanted gold.

Dreamily listening to the wild weird song, Bilbo is strangely moved by urges he hardly knew he possessed. "As they sang, the Hobbit felt the love of beautiful things made by hands and by cunning and by magic moving through him, a fierce and a jealous love, the desire of the hearts of Dwarves. Then something Tookish woke up inside him, and he wished to go and see the great mountains, and hear the pine-trees and the waterfalls, and explore the caves, and wear a sword instead of a walking stick."

So he goes off, jogging over mountain trails on ponyback, accompanying thirteen grim Dwarves and one old Wizard, to face a terrible dragon and dangers he cannot even imagine. It seems that in the days of Thorin's grandfather, the Dwarves from the North came down to dwell under the Lonely Mountain, which they mined and tunneled into great halls which they filled with a mighty hoard of gold and gems. But the hoard aroused the dragon, Smaug, for (as everyone knows) dragons love nothing more than to find or seize a treasure and guard it for ages. This particular one, Smaug, "a most specially greedy, strong and wicked worm," fell upon the Dwarves and drove them away or slew most of them. The survivors went into exile but never forgot the loss of their great halls under the Mountain; and now, with the aid of Bilbo Baggins, Esq., a mild, peace-loving Hobbit of the Shire, and Gandalf, a wandering Wizard interested in quixotic ventures, they intend to slay the dragon and regain their mountainous realm.

It makes quite a story. They cross the Misty Mountains, narrowly escaping the clutches of an oafish, quarrelsome band of Trolls; encounter a merry, singing troop of Elves; and eventually reach the edge of the Wild, where stands the Last Homely House of the West, the house of Elrond, who is "as noble and as fair in face as an elf-lord, as strong as a warrior, as wise as a wizard, as venerable as a king of dwarves."

From the house of Elrond, where they rest briefly, the party continues on its quest. While crossing a pass over the Misty Mountains, the travelers are attacked by a band of goblins,* Bilbo becomes parted from his comrades and an incident occurs which is later proved to be of some importance. In fact, if it had not been for this minor incident, the whole story of *The Hobbit* would probably have only earned "a passing footnote in history," as the Professor says.

Strayed afar and lost for a time, Bilbo wanders into caverns under the mountains, and there—groping through the darkness—he finds a ring which he slips into his pocket. A bit later, on a rock island in the midst of a cold black lake he encounters a loathsome, degraded little creature who calls himself Gollum. This repulsive little creature has lived here alone in the darkness and cold for many years, catching fish and eating them raw. His one joy was a secret treasure he called his "birthday present," a magic gold ring that makes its wearer invisible. It was the only thing Gollum loved—his "precious"—and, of course, it was this ring that Bilbo had found and slipped into his pocket.

Gollum might have attacked Bilbo had it not been for the bright Elvish sword he carried. So, to gain time, Gollum and Bilbo play a riddle game, which Bilbo wins by a trick. The cunning little Gollum promises that if Bilbo asks a riddle which Gollum can not answer, he will lead him to a way out of the caverns, but if he stumps Bilbo, he will kill and eat him. In the end Bilbo puts his hand in his pocket and comes upon the ring he had picked up and forgotten, and he cries out, "What have I got in my pocket?" Gollum cannot guess, and Bilbo forces the unhappy creature to keep his word. But Gollum's heart was

---

* In *The Hobbit* Professor Tolkien calls these creatures, the servants of Mordor, "goblins"; in *LOTR* he uses the Elvish word "Orc" for their kind.

black and rotten and treacherous, and he creeps away
in the dark and discovers that his birthday present, his
"precious," was not in the hidey-hole where he had left
it. Gollum realizes how Bilbo tricked him and scram-
bles back to murder the Hobbit. But as Bilbo flees, the
ring slips onto his finger and he is rendered invisible.
Overhearing Gollum weeping and babbling to his lost
"precious," Bilbo comes to understand that this is a
Ring of Power. With its spell he eludes the slimy
clutches of Gollum and escapes out of the mountain,
although the vengeful little monster shrieks after him,
"Thief! Thief! Baggins! We hates it for ever!"

Bilbo rejoins his comrades and for some peculiar,
guilty reason does not tell them the whole story about
the ring. Gandalf, however, is not fooled by his inno-
cent story; the old enchanter knows all about Rings of
Power, and although they are soon caught up in the
completion of their adventure and have no time for
further discussion, he continues in later years to be curious about the Ring and to keep an eye on Bilbo.

Indeed, the whirl of events is so swift from here to
the end of *The Hobbit* that the sequence of events can
only be briefly summarized. As they press on to the
Lonely Mountain, the travelers are attacked by wild
Wargs, have a difficult time with the goblins, from
whom they are rescued by friendly eagles, and survive
a grisly encounter with enormous spiders in the dark,
mysterious paths of Mirkwood, greatest of the forests
of the North.

They come to the Mountain, and Bilbo sneaks in to
catch a glimpse of the dragon: "Smaug lay, with wings
folded like an immeasurable bat . . . a vast red-golden
dragon, fast asleep; beneath him, under all his limbs
and his huge coiled tail, and about him on all sides

40

stretching away across the unseen floors, lay countless piles of precious things, gold wrought and unwrought, gems and jewels and silver red-stained in the fiery light . . . his long pale belly crusted with gems and fragments of gold from his long lying on his costly bed." Fascinated, Bilbo stares at the tremendous monster and notes that the dragon's softer underparts are armored in hard gems—"a waistcoat of diamonds"; and he also notices that there is a large patch in the hollow of Smaug's left breast that is bare of gems.

Smaug rouses from slumber and Bilbo engages him in conversation. The dragon is enraged, for he cannot see his invisible tormentor. He roars, and "the light of his eyes lit the hall from floor to ceiling like scarlet lightning." The dragon mocks at the coming of the Dwarves: "Revenge! The King under the Mountain is dead and where are his kin that dare seek revenge? . . . I laid low the warriors of old and their like is not in the world today. Then I was but young and tender. Now I am old and strong, strong," the dragon gloats. "My armour is like tenfold shields, my teeth are swords, my claws spears, the shock of my tail a thunderbolt, my wings a hurricane, and my breath death!"

The dragon, fully roused to lashing anger, leaves the Mountain to ravish a nearby town of Men. Tolkien describes the scene vividly:

A whirring noise was heard. A red light touched the points of standing rocks. The dragon came. They had barely time to fly back to the tunnel, pulling and dragging in their bundles, when Smaug came hurtling from the North, licking the mountainsides with flame, beating his great wings with a noise like a roaring wind. His hot breath shrivelled the grass before the door, and drove in through the crack they had left and scorched them as they lay hid. Flickering fires leaped up and black rock-shadows danced. Then darkness fell as he passed again. The ponies screamed with terror, burst their ropes and galloped wildly off. The dragon swooped and turned to pursue them, and was gone.

It is one of the Men, Bard the archer, who slays Smaug. He sinks a black arrow through the unprotected place in the hollow of the dragon's left breast, the very spot that Bilbo had noticed.

Thus Thorin became King under the Mountain and regained the treasure of his ancestors, although there was some trouble with various groups of claimants for this or that portion of the hoard, and for a time he was actually besieged in the Mountain by Men and Elves and had to summon his cousin Dáin for help in raising the siege.

Eventually, however, these last few matters are settled in mutual amity, more or less, and the characters of the story part and go their several ways. Thus Bilbo returns again to his beloved Shire with his share of the treasure and with the Ring.

This book, *The Hobbit,* serves as a novel-length prelude to the trilogy itself, although it can be read and fully enjoyed on its own terms. But it sets the scene and establishes the needed background for the themes dealt with more fully in *LOTR,* which is the story of the Ring and of the quest and war and adventures that surround it once it has been discovered to be the great Ring of Power, the One Ring, key talisman in a tremendous struggle between the forces of Light and the Powers of Darkness.

5.

The Story of
The Fellowship of the Ring

> The mountain air is fresh at the dusk of day;
> The flying birds two by two return.
> In these things there lies a deep meaning;
> Yet when we would express it, words suddenly fail us.
> *T'ao Ch'ien* (Arthur Waley translation)

~~~~~~~~~~~~~~~~~~~~~~~~~~~~~~

The first volume of the trilogy is called *The Fellowship of the Ring*. It opens sixty years after Bilbo's return to the Shire. Now a very, very old Hobbit, he decides to celebrate his one hundred and eleventh birthday in a most unusual manner indeed: by vanishing. Bilbo has decided to go off for a last holiday—in fact, to go away for good. "I want to see the wild country again before I die, and the Mountains," he tells Gandalf. He has adopted young Frodo Baggins as his heir and to Frodo he leaves Bag End and the Ring. In the middle of a perfectly spectacular birthday party, therefore, Bilbo announces to his old friends and neighbors that he is leaving the Shire never to return; he slips the Ring on his finger and disappears right before their eyes.

Gandalf, of course, was involved with the whole plan from the beginning, and he makes sure that the old Hobbit does indeed pass the Ring on to Frodo. For Gandalf has become increasingly worried about this seemingly unimportant talisman, suspecting that it is a certain very famous ring—the great Ring of Sauron in fact, the "One Ring" which the evil lord created in an earlier age. As yet, he does nothing but waits and watches.

Some years later it becomes necessary for Gandalf to speak of his suspicions to Frodo. Rumors of strange things abroad in the world and the coming of dark and difficult days are whispered. The evil power that had originally centered in the dark, gloomy forest of Mirkwood has been driven out by the White Council, a group of powerful magicians and Elven lords who work for the forces of good in the world. But evil is hard to destroy; the dark power reappears in the eastern land of Mordor, its ancient home. And now its strength is on the rise. Bands of cunningly armed Trolls are seen; there are rumors of Dragons; the Dark Tower has been rebuilt and is again the stronghold of a grim power. To the east and south there are wars and spreading fear.

Gandalf makes a rare visit to the Shire and tells Frodo of his suspicions. He conducts a test which proves the Ring to be one of the great and terrible Rings of Power. They were made ages ago, three of them for the Elves and seven for the Dwarves, nine for mortal Men, and one for the Dark Lord himself; and the Ring Bilbo found and Frodo now owns is the One:

> One Ring to rule them all, One Ring to find them.
> One Ring to bring them all and in the darkness bind them
> In the Land of Mordor where the Shadows lie.

Yes, this is the One Ring that was the center of Sauron's power when in an earlier age he strove with Elves and Men for world mastery. It was Gil-galad the Elven-king and Elendil of Westernesse who overthrew him of old, and they perished in the deed. But Isildur, Elendil's son, cut the Ring from Sauron's hand when he was crushed. The Ring was lost soon after, when Isildur was waylaid by Orcs and his people slain. He leaped into the great river Anduin and the Ring slipped from his finger, and the Orcs saw him and slew him with arrows, and the Ring was lost. But that which has been crushed does not stay crushed forever; and that which is lost may be found. Thus, although Sauron was vanquished and his spirit fled away and remained hidden for long years, gathering strength, his shadow again took shape in Mirkwood and had now returned to Mordor. And the Ring was discovered by a creature called Déagol, one of a clever-handed and quiet-footed little people akin to Hobbit-kind who lived along the banks of Anduin. Déagol found the Ring inside a freshly killed fish, but his friend Sméagol was watching and lusted for the Ring and slew him to get it. The Ring tempted and perverted him, as it does to all who wear it and use it long enough. Armed with its powers of invisibility, Sméagol became malicious and took to thieving and to going about muttering to himself and gurgling in a nasty way, "Gollum, Gollum"; eventually his folk turned against him and cursed him and drove him from their burrows. He took to calling himself Gollum and wandered up the river and came into the mountains and found a home in the dark depths and caves where Bilbo later discovered him.

Gandalf reveals all this to Frodo because Gollum still hungers for the Ring and searches for it, and his searches have led him even within the borders of Mordor; hence the Dark Power, newly risen and greatly weakened from the loss of its Ring, has thus been apprised of Hobbits and the Shire. Black Riders are loping about the edges of the Shire, and it will not be long before they enter the Hobbits' country in force to gain possession of the Ring for their grim Master.

Frodo is alarmed and dismayed. If he remains in the Shire, he will lead the agents of the cruel Enemy among his people. He offers the Ring to Gandalf, but the magician recoils in dread, saying, "No! With that power I should have power too great and terrible. And over me the Ring would gain a power still greater and more deadly. Do not tempt me! For I do not wish to become like the Dark Lord himself. Yet the way of the Ring to my heart is by pity, pity for weakness and the desire of strength to do good. Do not tempt me! I dare not take it, not even to keep it safe, unused. The wish to wield it would be too great for my strength."

The Ring cannot be kept hidden for long from the dark adversary, but it can be destroyed. Alas, it can only be destroyed if it is cast into the fiery furnaces wherein it was made, and that place is in Mordor itself. Gandalf advises Frodo to take to the road and stay away from the Shire, to strike for Rivendell, where the house of Elrond stands. There the White Council may be able to suggest a plan.

One dark night, therefore, Frodo and the Ring leave the Shire, accompanied by three of his young Hobbit friends, Samwise (Sam) Gamgee, Meriadoc (Merry) Brandybuck, and Peregrin (Pippin) Took. Their perilous journey leads them through the wooded country about the Shire, where they have a narrow brush with the Black Riders and encounter a friendly band of Elves. They are saved from an evil tree by a jolly, singing, happy being named Tom Bombadil. Neither Man, Hobbit, Dwarf, nor Elf, Tom is the embodiment of utter goodness and old as time itself. As he puts it:

> "Eldest, that's what I am. . . . Tom was here before the river and the trees; Tom remembers the first raindrop and the first acorn. When the Elves passed westward, Tom was here already. . . . He knew the dark under the stars when it was fearless—before the Dark Lord came from Outside."

After a grim scene where the Hobbits are trapped by barrow weights inside an ancient mound, from which Tom rescues them, they reach Bree and take haven in an inn called The Prancing Pony. There they notice a strange Man watching them.

> A strange-looking, weather-beaten man, sitting in the shadows near the wall, was also listening intently to the hobbit-talk. He had a tall tankard in front of him, and was smoking a long-stemmed pipe, curiously carved. His legs were stretched out before him, showing high boots of supple leather that fitted him well, but had seen much wear and were now caked with mud. A travel-stained cloak of heavy dark-green cloth was drawn closely about him, and in spite of the heat of the room he wore a hood that overshadowed his face; but the gleam of his eyes could be seen as he watched the hobbits.

The landlord tells Frodo that the stranger is "one of the wandering folk—Rangers we call them. What his right name is I've never heard: but he's known round here as Strider." The landlord also passes on to Frodo a letter from Gandalf that tells the Hobbits they can trust "a Man, lean, dark, tall, by some called Strider," whose real name is Aragorn. The letter also quotes a cryptic bit of verse that in part goes:

> From the ashes a fire shall be woken.
> A light from the shadows shall spring;
> Renewed shall be blade that was broken,
> The crownless again shall be king.

With Strider the Ranger as their guide, they depart for Rivendell, where Gandalf hopes to meet them. Strider (or Aragorn, as he now calls himself) tells them tales of olden lore, of Gil-galad and Elendil and of Eärendil who wed Elwing the White and begat the kings of Númenor, an old name for Westernesse. Although attacked by Black Riders, who strike Frodo senseless with a blast of magic, the party arrive safely at Rivendell. Gandalf is there and tells Frodo that Aragorn is one of the race of great Kings who came from over the Sea in olden days, the Dúnedain, the Men of the West.

The Council convenes to consider the problem of the Ring. Hither are come emissaries of the Elves, such as Glorfindel, a great Elven Prince—"tall and straight; his hair was of shining gold, his face fair and young and fearless and full of joy; his eyes were bright and keen, and his voice like music; on his brow sat wisdom, and in his hand was strength." Hither, too, has come Glóin, one of the Dwarves who accompanied Bilbo in *The Hobbit,* and his son, Gimli. And a strange Elf clad in green and brown, named Legolas —a messenger from his father, Thranduil the King of the Elves in Northern Mirkwood. Seated a little apart from the others is a tall Man with a fair and noble face, dark-haired and gray-eyed, proud and stern of glance, Boromir from the south. Elrond Halfelven speaks of Sauron and the Rings of Power and of their making in the Second Age of the world, long ago.

Of Númenor he spoke, its glory and its fall, and the return of the Kings of Men to Middle-earth out of the deeps of the Sea, borne upon the wings of storm. Then Elendil the Tall and his mighty sons, Isildur and Anarion, became great lords: and of the North-realm they made in Arnor, and the South-realm in Gondor about the mouths of Anduin. But Sauron of Mordor assailed them, and they made the Last Alliance of Elves and Men, and the hosts of Gil-galad and Elendil were mustered in Arnor.

And Elrond reveals his incredible age; for while the Elves are immortal, even those who are but Halfelven live to amazing longevities:

"My memory reaches back even to the Elder Days. Eärendil was my sire, who was born in Gondolin before its fall; and my mother was Elwing, daughter of Dior, son of Luthien of Doriath. I have seen three ages in the West of the world, and many defeats, and many fruitless victories. I was the herald of Gil-galad and marked with his host. I was at the Battle of Dagorlad before the Black Gate of Mordor, where we had the mastery: for the Spear of Gil-galad and the Sword of Elendil, Aiglos and Narsil, none could withstand. I beheld the last combat on the slopes of Orodruin, where Gil-galad died, and Elendil fell, and Narsil broke beneath him; but Sauron himself was overthrown, and Isildur cut the Ring from his hand." *

Elrond tells that after the war the Men of Westernesse were diminished. The folk of Arnor dwindled and were devoured by foes. In the south, however, the

---

* As explained in Chapter 3, I suspect that the plot of *The Silmarillion* (the prequel to *LOTR*, which is laid in the Second Age) will be concerned chiefly with the Last Alliance and the war against Sauron, culminating in this scene in which the Ring is taken from Sauron during the last combat on the slopes of Orodruin the Mountain of Fire. The Ring should have been thrown into the volcanic mountain at that time; that it was not is the fault of Isildur and the cause of the struggle which forms the plot of *The Lord of the Rings*.

realm of Gondor long endured and even grew in splendor, recalling something of lost Númenor in the days of its might before it fell.

The Council continues. Frodo sees Arwen, daughter of Elrond, a woman of unearthly, serene beauty. He hears many tales of the Second Age. Glóin reveals that the Dark Lord has sent embassies to the Dwarves, calling for mutual friendship and promising much. They speak of Gondor near the gateway to Mordor, land of the shadows, Gondor which stands guardian to the Black Gate and of how it prospered since the Second Age.

"High towers that people built, and strong places, and havens of many ships; and the winged crown of the Kings of Men was held in awe by folk of many tongues. Their chief city was Osgiliath, Citadel of the Stars, through the midst of which the River flowed. And Minas Ithil they built, Tower of the Rising Moon, eastward upon a shoulder of the Mountain of Shadow; and westward at the feet of the White Mountain, Minas Anor they made, Tower of the Setting Sun. There in the courts of the King grew a white tree, from the seed of that tree which Isildur brought over the deep waters, and the seed of that tree before came from Eressëa and before that out of the Uttermost West in the Day before days when the world was young."

At this, Boromir the Man from the South rises to tell his tale. He has come from Gondor and tells how the South-realm still stands as the bulwark of the West, holding at bay the wild folk of the East and the forces of the Black Land of Mordor. Mordor is on the rise; the Dark Lord has made alliances with the Easterlings and the cruel Haradrim. Still Gondor stands, but not for long. Its allies have fallen away. Those who shelter behind the bulwark of Gondor give much praise but little aid in time of trouble. Only from the country of Rohan now will any ride to Gondor with aid of arms. But Boromir is come to the house of Elrond, not for warriors, but for wisdom. A prophetic dream has come to the Stewards of Gondor, saying that a Sword that was broken must be found again in Imladris: a troubling dream, in which the skies over the East darkened but a pale light lingered in the West. Denethor, Lord of Minas Tirith, has dispatched Boromir, his son, to Elrond for advice, since "Imladris" is an old name for the place where Elrond dwells. At this, Aragorn the Ranger stands and casts his sword upon the table, crying that this is the Sword that was broken. It is revealed that Aragorn is the descendent of Isildur, chief of the Dúnedain in the North. The Sword is that which broke under Elendil in the last combat. His heirs have treasured it from that day to this, for it was said of old that the Sword would be made whole again when the Ring was found in time to come. Aragorn asks ringingly if the day has come when the House of Elendil is to return to power in Gondor.

The White Council continues. Gandalf reveals that Saruman the White, a great magician and chief of Gandalf's own order, has been corrupted and turned traitor, tempted by the lure of the Ring and by envy of the power of the Dark Lord. The Ring must be destroyed. Neither Glorfindel nor Gandalf nor Elrond dare take the burden. Who, then, is the chosen Ring bearer?

No one answered. The noon-bell rang. Still no one spoke. Frodo glanced at all the faces, but they were not turned to him. All the Council sat with downcast eyes, as if in deep thought. A great dread fell on him, as if he was awaiting the pronouncement of some doom that he had long foreseen and vainly hoped might after all never be spoken. An overwhelming longing to rest and remain at peace by Bilbo's side in Rivendell filled all his heart. At last with an effort he spoke, and wondered to hear his own words, as if some other will was using his small voice.

"I will take the Ring," he said, "though I do not know the way."

It is decided. But Frodo will not bear the dreadful burden unaccompanied. A Fellowship is formed to go by his side and help him against the perils that lie in his path. Nine will go on the Quest: Legolas the Elf, armed with his bow; Gimli the Dwarf in his mailshirt, bearing his broad-bladed axe; Gandalf the Grey, armed with his staff and with the sword Glamdring at his side; Aragorn, bearing the Sword of Elendil, which elvish smiths have repaired and to which Aragorn has now given the new name of Andúril, Flame of the West; Boromir of Gondor; Pippin, Merry, and Sam, armed with their own swords; and Frodo the Ring bearer, to whom old Bilbo gives a suit of Dwarvish mail and the sword Sting.

They set forth and pass through dark forests and swamps. Beset by evil Wargs, they seek passage through the subterranean realm of Moria, where was once a great kingdom of the Dwarves. There in the dark underground ways they are ambushed by Orcs and flee to a narrow bridge across a mighty chasm, fighting their way to freedom through the Orcs. Even a great Troll cannot halt them, but then comes upon them an enemy most fearful indeed. "Ai! Ai!" wails Legolas in despair. *"A Balrog* is come!" Gandalf sags in despair. "A Balrog," he mutters. "Now I understand." He falters and leans heavily on his staff. "What an evil fortune! And I am already weary."

Rousing himself, the old Wizard drives them across the bridge. "Fly! This is a foe beyond any of you. I must hold the narrow way. Fly!" Then:

The Balrog reached the bridge. Gandalf stood in the middle of the span, leaning on the staff in his left hand, but in his other hand Glamdring gleamed, cold and white. His enemy halted again, facing him, and the shadow about it reached out like two vast wings. It raised the whip, and the thongs whined and cracked. Fire came from its nostrils. But Gandalf stood firm.

"You cannot pass," he said. The Orcs stood still, and a dead silence fell. "I am a servant of the Secret Fire, wielder of the flame of Anor. You cannot pass."

They battle there, on the narrow way over the abyss. The Balrog sets its flaming red sword against the cold fire of Glamdring, but the red sword is shattered apart in molten fragments. Gandalf staggers back, then regains his stance again. "You cannot pass," he repeats. The Balrog comes fully upon the bridge, lashing its whip. "He cannot stand alone!" Aragorn cries suddenly and runs back, shouting, "Elendil! Elendil! I am with you, Gandalf!" "Gondor! Gondor!" Boromir booms, and leaps after him to the old Wizard's aid.

At that moment Gandalf lifted his staff, and crying aloud he smote the bridge before him. The staff broke asunder and fell from his hand. A blinding sheet of white flame sprang up. The bridge cracked. Right at the Balrog's feet it broke . . . and crashed into the gulf. With a terrible cry the Balrog fell forward, and its shadow plunged down and vanished. But even as it fell it swung its whip, and the thongs lashed and curled about the wizard's knees, dragging him to the brink. He staggered and fell, grasping vainly at the stone, and slid into the abyss. "Fly, you fools!" he cried, and was gone.

Thus passes Gandalf the Grey. And darkness comes

down. Weeping with pity and horror, the Fellowship stagger forward, urged on by Aragorn, who now assumes leadership. They emerge at last into open air and the light of day. They flee on and find refuge in Lothlorien, where the friendly Queen, Galadriel, gives them shelter for a time. When they depart, she gives them a crystal vial of pure water from her Fountain, which will prove of aid when need has come for it.

Now that Gandalf is gone, the company misses his wise leadership. Divisions spring up between them and they quarrel, remembering old enmities between Elf and Dwarf. Boromir disputes the leadership of Aragorn and argues that they should bear the Ring to Gondor first. When Frodo goes apart to think things through, Boromir secretly seeks him out and strives to wrest the Ring from him, first by cunning words and then by sheer force. Frodo flies, terrified at the greed in the face of the man he had thought a friend. He realizes now just how great the burden of the Ring truly is, that it sows envy and temptation among all those close to the Ring bearer. He runs off into the wilderness accompanied only by Sam, and they come to the borders of the Dark Land, where they must go forward alone.

Searching for Frodo, the Fellowship breaks up, never again to be reassembled. The long Quest is now almost over. The great War is about to begin.

6.

The Story of
The Two Towers

How fare the gods? How fare the elves?
All Jotunheim groans, the gods are at council;
Loud roar the dwarfs by the doors of stone,
The masters of the rocks . . . would you know yet more?
The Elder Edda, Voluspo, 48

The second volume of the trilogy is called *The Two Towers.* The book opens on a scene immediately following the closing scenes of *The Fellowship of the Ring.* Searching for Frodo and Sam, the Fellowship splits up. Boromir, repenting of his ill deed, comes to the aid of the two younger Hobbits, Pippin and Merry, who have become separated from the others and are lost in the woods. When a band of Orcs sets upon them, Boromir battles mightily, sounding his horn. Though his last stand is a glorious one, for all his valor he falls, riddled with arrows.

Thus passes the heir of Denethor, Steward of Gondor, and thus does he make recompense for his betrayal of the Quest.

The others come upon the battle scene. Pippin and Merry have vanished; presumably, they were carried off by the Orcs. Searching the bodies of the fallen for some clue, the rest discover that some among the bodies wore unfamiliar armor and strange accouterments. Their helms bear an unfamiliar emblem, the sign of a White Hand, and an S-rune, which must stand for the ambivalent Magician of the West, Saruman the White, chief of Gandalf's own order. They assume, correctly, that Saruman has become corrupted by the lust for power and is searching for the Ring bearer for his own dark purposes.

Aragorn the Man, Gimli the Dwarf, and Legolas the Elf are all that now remain of the Fellowship. For want of any better plan, they follow the trail of the Orcs who took captive Pippin and Merry. They enter the land of the Rohirrim and encounter the warriors of Rohan, who stop and question them suspiciously. The Rohirrim are spear-tall and stalwart horsemen with pale, flaxen hair, painted shields, and coats of burnished mail. In these troubled and uncertain times, with wars and rumors of war to every hand, with the power of the Enemy growing from day to day, mysterious travelers are not welcome. Aragorn talks with a lord of the Mark of Rohan named Éomer. He convinces the warrior that they are friends, and Éomer tells that he and his horsemen set upon and crushed the same party of Orcs that Aragorn is following. They found no Hobbits among them. Éomer gives them horses and returns to report to his king, while Aragorn and the others continue toward the ancient Fangorn forest to search for the two lost Hobbits.

The scene then shifts to Merry and Pippin and tells how they escaped from their Orc captors and fled to take shelter in Fangorn—a very great and a very ancient wood of ill-repute—before the Rohirrim came upon and overwhelmed the horde of Saruman. Wan-

dering in the dark woods they encounter a strange and
kindly being called Treebeard, of an almost forgotten
race known as Ents, the "Shepherds of the Trees."
Wise, humorous, philosophical, slow of speech, the
friendly old Ent finds the sprightly young Hobbits very
peculiar. They find him even more strange:

> They found that they were looking at a most extraordi-
> nary face. It belonged to a large Man-like, almost Troll-
> like figure, at least fourteen feet high, very sturdy, with a
> tall head, and hardly any neck. Whether it was clad in
> stuff like green and grey bark, or whether that was its
> hide, was difficult to say. At any rate, the arms, at a short
> distance from the trunk, were not wrinkled, but covered
> with a brown, smooth skin. The large feet had seven toes
> each. The lower part of the long face was covered with a
> sweeping grey beard, bushy, almost twiggy at the roots,
> thin and mossy at the ends. But at the moment the hob-
> bits noted little but the eyes. These deep eyes were now
> surveying them, slow and solemn, but very penetrating.
> They were brown, shot with a green light.

Treebeard's slow, thoughtful speech reveals him as
grave and solemn and very ancient. He is one of the
most totally original and completely fascinating characters in the entire trilogy, a creation of the imagination to rank with Tom Bombadil in the first volume.
He takes the young Hobbits home with him and feeds
them. From Orc talk they overheard during their cap-
tivity, the Hobbits tell him that Saruman has become
wicked, a fact Treebeard had begun to suspect. But far
from joining on the side of Sauron of Mordor, the
White Magician is attempting to set himself up as a
new power in the land. Treebeard is slow to anger, but
he becomes solemnly enraged against Saruman, for the
Lord of Orthanc has been felling trees on the edges of
Fangorn and is bringing Orcs into the woods. This for-

est of Fangorn is Treebeard's own demesne; its trees are under his protection; with his fellow Ents, he cares for them and tends their needs, as a gardener might tend his plants. He rouses the other Ents, and they march upon Isengard, the tower of Saruman.

Meanwhile, their search for the two lost Hobbits has led Aragorn and his comrades into the same forest. During the night they catch a glimpse of an old man whose hat shades his features, watching them from the shadows. They fear this to be Saruman, but he vanishes when they call out to him. The next day, as they continue their search,

> Aragorn looked and beheld a bent figure moving slowly. It was not far away. It looked like an old beggar-man, walking wearily, leaning on a rough staff. His head was bowed, and he did not look towards them. In other lands they would have greeted him with kind words; but now they stood silent, each feeling a strange expectancy: something was approaching that held a hidden power—or menace.

Beneath the tatters of his gray robes they catch a glimpse of *white* garments! Surely it must be the dreaded Saruman. The old man stops and speaks to them in veiled, soft-voiced, ambiguous words, still concealing his features from them. When the short-tempered Gimli challenges him with the name of Saruman and makes for him,

> The old man was too quick for him. He sprang to his feet and leaped to the top of a large rock. There he stood, grown suddenly tall, towering above them. His hood and his grey rags were flung away. His white garments shone. He lifted up his staff, and Gimli's axe leaped from his grasp and fell ringing to the ground. The sword of Aragorn, stiff in his motionless hand, blazed with a sudden fire. Legolas gave a great shout and shot an arrow high

into the air: it vanished in a flash of flame. "Mithrandir!"

They all gazed at him. His hair was white as snow in the sunshine; and gleaming white was his robe; the eyes under his deep brows were bright, piercing as the rays of the sun; power was in his hand. Between wonder, joy, and fear they stood and found no words to say.

Indeed it is Gandalf, Gandalf returned to dwell among the living once again, after terrible trials. Still shaken by awe, they tell him of all that has happened since he was taken from them there on the narrow bridge across the abyss, when the lash of the Balrog dragged him into the great gulf and they went on alone. He tells them little of his strange experiences in that dark realm whereof the living know so little.

"Long I fell, and he [the Balrog] with me. His fire was about me. I was burned. Then we plunged into the deep water and all was dark. Cold it was as the tide of death: almost it froze my heart. . . . Yet it has a bottom, beyond light and knowledge. Thither I came at last, to the uttermost foundations of stone. He was with me still. His fire was quenched, but now he was a thing of slime, stronger than a strangling snake. We fought far under the living earth, where time is not counted. Ever he clutched me, and ever I hewed him, till at last he fled into dark tunnels. They were not made by Durin's folk, Gimli son of Glóin. Far, far below the deepest delvings of the Dwarves, the world is gnawed by nameless things."

In a slow, dreaming voice, Gandalf further tells of how he pursued his enemy, the Balrog, and followed him through the depths of Moria by the Endless Stair to the top of the highest peak of the mountains. There, amid dazzling sun on white snow, they fought anew.

"I threw down my enemy, and he fell from the high place and broke the mountain-side where he smote it in his ruin. Then darkness took me, and I strayed out of thought

59

and time, and I wandered far on roads that I will not tell. Naked I was sent back—for a brief time, until my task is done."

Gandalf does not say it (neither does Tolkien, in so many words), but the implication is that Gandalf passed into death and beyond, returning to Middle-earth strengthened and purified and renewed, now far stronger than before. He is Gandalf the Grey no more —now he is the White. And he has yet many great deeds of worth to do in the affairs of the world, ere he may leave it again.

They ride first into Rohan, Gandalf mounted on Shadowfax, a great steed without peer. They find Théoden, King of the Mark, old and sunk in dreams, his manhood sapped and his mind poisoned with suspicion by the sly, cunning words spun by his servant, Grima Wormtongue, who has entrapped him in a web of hints and subtle accusations and who has himself become great in the land. They fence with words, but Gandalf has little time to waste. He reveals himself in the splendor of his might and hurls Grima to the floor in a blast of magic. Then he leads the old king out into the light and open air, and his winged words drive the fogs and shadows from Théoden's mind, infusing him with new strength and vigor.

Théoden summons his warriors, and they ride out. At Helm's Deep they are entrapped by Orcs, and a mighty battle is fought wherein both Legolas and Gimli acquit themselves splendidly in the fight, from which Gandalf brings them forth with victory. Then, swift as flying hooves can carry them, they speed to Isengard to confront Saruman. For Grima has been unmasked as an agent of the White Hand, and Théoden has banished him from the realm. They come upon

Orthanc, magic citadel of the traitorous magician, and find it has become a beleaguered fortress.

For Treebeard and the Ents have broken the power of Saruman, slain or driven off his servants, and laid all his works in waste. The magician himself (together with Grima Wormtongue, as is later revealed) are besieged within. Gandalf confronts the White Magician, whose silken tongue almost beguiles even the grim and vengeful King of the Mark. But Gandalf faces him down, reveals that he has now ascended to higher rank, breaks Saruman's magic staff, and deposes him from the order. Grima, striking like a snake from ambush, hurls a stone at Gandalf. Gandalf is not struck and discovers to his delight that the stone is one that Saruman would not willingly lose. It is a *palantir,* a magic crystal of great power, the instrument by which Orthanc and the Dark Tower of Barad-dûr (the "two towers" of the title) were linked together in communication in earlier days.

After bidding farewell to Treebeard and settling down for the night, the unwary Pippin makes the mistake of peering within the crystal and is seized temporarily by the mind of Sauron. He takes no hurt from the dreadful experience, and luckily he knows little that would be of value to the Enemy.

Gandalf rides at top speed toward Minas Tirith, chief city of Gondor, hoping to arrive before the tides of war break against the bastions of that land.

The scene next switches to Frodo and Sam, who are making their way along the borders of Mordor. While passing through mountainous country, they come upon the Gollum skulking and sneaking about. The wretched little creature is so pitiful that Frodo shows mercy to him although Sam stoutly argues that the

treacherous little snake should not be trusted. Frodo,
however, persists; he treats Sméagol gently and with
sympathy. Suffering from the crushing burden of the
Ring, he knows something of the agony and degrada-
tion that has tormented the poor little creature all
these years. As for Gollum, it is so long since any living thing has regarded him with any emotion less than
loathing (much less with pity) that he responds to
Frodo's kindness fawningly and guides the Hobbits
across the marshes.

These scenes, wherein Gollum responds with pitiful
eagerness to the slightest bit of kindness and trust, are
most touching and are beautifully handled.

Before the Black Gate that leads into Mordor the
group encounters troops from Minas Tirith led by Faramir, a Captain of Gondor, with whom they exchange
news, parting at length to attempt entry to the Black
Land by means of a dark tunnel through the mountains. But this lightless cavern is the dark and fetid lair
of Shelob, a frightful spider monster of unnatural size
and vile disposition. Sam recalls the vial of water from
the Elf Queen's fountain and the words Galadriel
spake when she gave it to them—"A light when all
other lights go out!" He lifts the glass, and its pure radiance drives Shelob back into the further recesses of
her abode. They press forward, hewing a path through
the thick, clotted tangle of webs that block their passage.

Then she comes upon them again, and a desperate
battle is waged in the foul darkness. Gollum turns on
Sam, whom he has never liked (probably because the
stout Hobbit never trusted him and argued against
Frodo's putting any reliance on the miserable little
creature). Gollum is beaten off and flees. Sam turns to

assist Frodo, and discovers to his incredulous horror
that his master has been stung with the spider's poison
sting and is seemingly dead. Weeping, Sam flings himself on Shelob in a burst of heroism. Galadriel's phial
blazes up with intolerable radiance, and Sam's sword
cripples the blinded Shelob. The maimed thing crawls
away to seek her lonely, hidden nest.

Now Sam—poor, simple, trustworthy Sam—must
decide what to do. Must he—can he—assume the burden of the Ring and go forward on his own, to complete the Quest that Frodo did not live to finish? That
would mean he must go off and leave poor Frodo's
body untended, to sleep forever in this foul place.
Alas, he knows he must do it. He is the last of the Fellowship, and the responsibility has devolved upon his
sturdy shoulders: he must go forward so long as
strength lasts within him. Sobbing, he tenderly removes
the Ring from Frodo's body and goes to the end of the
underground passage.

A passing patrol of Orcs comes upon the Hobbit's
corpse. They puzzle as to whose body it is and how it
came to this place. They bear it away, and Sam lingers
near them. Putting on the Ring, he becomes invisible
so as to follow closely. As they near their fortress, he
overhears a bit of dialogue between two Orcs that
strikes him reeling with horror.

One Orc argues there is no reason to turn the body
over to their superiors at Lugburz, since it is dead.

"What Lugburz will do with such stuff I can't guess. He
might as well go in the pot."

"You fool," snarled Shagrat. "You've been talking very
clever, but there's a lot you don't know, though most
other folk do. You'll be for the pot or for Shelob, if you
don't take care. Carrion! Is that all you know of Her La-
dyship? When she binds with cords, she's after meat. She

doesn't eat dead meat, nor suck cold blood. This fellow isn't dead!"

Overcome with horror, Sam realizes the spider's venom only paralyzed Frodo. Had he not lingered to listen to the Orc's chatter, he might very well have gone off and left Frodo at the mercy of Shelob's hunger, if the spider monster survived the wounds of his sword and the stabbing rays of Galadriel's phial. If not, the poor Hobbit's fate would have been even more grim: he would have lain paralyzed in the dark dens of Shelob until he starved to death.

He wavers, torn by indecision. What is he to do now? He must bear the Ring forward to the completion of the Quest—yet how can he go off and leave his helpless master, alive but devoid of the power of speech and movement, a captive in the hands of the cruel Enemy?

As Sam watches, Frodo's body is carried within the grim Orc fortress and the gates clang shut.

7.

The Story of
The Return of the King

All the gods
Are there, and all the powers of nameless worlds,
Vast, sceptred phantoms; heroes, men and beasts;
And Demogorgon, a tremendous gloom.
SHELLEY, *Prometheus Unbound*, Act 1, Scene 1

~~~~~~~~~~

The last volume of the trilogy is *The Return of the King*. As it opens, Gandalf and Pippin are riding like the wind for the beleaguered kingdom of Gondor. They arrive at its chief city, Minas Tirith, and are ushered into the presence of Denethor, Steward of Gondor. Gandalf warns the impulsive young Hobbit to watch his words when speaking to the cunning and subtle Lord Denethor, who springs from a lineage more proud and ancient even than Théoden and is as mighty a king, although he does not take that title but reigns, as it were, merely as the Steward of the lost king's realm. Gandalf obviously does not wish Denethor to have any advance notice of the forthcoming arrival of Aragorn, who will claim the vacant throne as the descendent of Gondor's lost kings. And he warns Pippin to watch his tongue when speaking of Boromir. " 'Do as I bid! It is scarcely wise when bringing the news of the death of his heir to a mighty lord to speak over much of the coming of one who will, if he comes, claim the kingship.' "

Even as Gandalf foresaw, Denethor closely questions the young Hobbit about the Fellowship and of the passing of Boromir. But the painful interview draws to a close at last. Moved by some strange impulse—perhaps a mingling of pity and admiration for the bitter, proud, and lonely old autocrat, now sonless —Pippin swears fealty to the Steward, and his service is accepted.

Pippin thereafter takes little part in the councils of the mighty who are making preparation for the coming conflict. He wanders about the city and makes new friends. After a time the brief interval of peace comes to an end. The war clouds break, the storm nears, and the great Captains of the Outlands arrive with their men to bolster the defenses of Gondor. Alas, their numbers are all too few. What if Rohan does not come?

We then return to Aragorn, Gimli, and Legolas where Gandalf left them to ride ahead to Gondor. They are still near the ruin of Saruman's citadel, Orthanc. But soon they, too, depart with Théoden for the mustering of the Rohirrim. To this gathering place also come Rangers, Aragorn's people from the North, to join the greatest of wars. They come bearing a precious gift from Arwen the daughter of Elrond Halfelven of Rivendell—the royal standard, of Gondor's King recreated.

In a scene that is obviously an intentional counterpart of that in which Pippin swore his oath to Denethor, the other young Hobbit, Merry, swears allegiance to Théoden, King of the Mark, and becomes an esquire of Rohan. Aragorn, Gimli, and Legolas the Elf part company with the Riders of Rohan as they are assembling. Aragorn has looked into the *palantir,* which is his right as Isildur's Heir and true owner of the magic stone. He has learned that war hovers at the gates of Gondor and that he must be there when the storm breaks. To await the completion of the mustering of the Rohirrim will delay him too long. The three comrades therefore take a perilous and ill-famed shortcut through the Paths of the Dead. They pass into the shadows under black Dwimorberg, the Haunted Mountain. Of their strange experiences in that realm Tolkien has little to say. The folk that once dwelt therein are accursed for an ancient sin. Aragorn's coming seems to liberate them from their punishment. When he and the others emerge, a shadowy company of the ancient dead ride with them.

In Gondor the war begins suddenly. Black sorcery casts a pall of gloom; the sun of morning does not shine and a nameless dread saps the strength of the defenders. The host of the enemy lay siege to the walls of Minas Tirith. Battles are fought there in the weird darkness. Doubts trouble the hearts of the valiant, and troubles spring up between the groups. Denethor quarrels with Gandalf and with his son, Faramir, the captain of the host who met Frodo at the borders of the Black Land and permitted him to depart. Denethor has an inkling of the thing Frodo carries, and he bitterly bemoans that it was not brought into Gondor, so that he might employ its power in the defense of the endangered realm. Denethor and his son Faramir part on a bitter note.

The war advances. The hosts of Mordor batter through the outer wall. The Lord of Barad-dûr, a ghost rider of the flying Nazgûl who had once been

King of Angmar long ago, leads the dark host. Gandalf calls him "a spear of terror in the hand of Sauron." In the unbroken gloom, amid the turmoil of battle, men's hearts beat low. But the swan knights of Dol Amroth break the enemy on either flank, and Gandalf, mounted on mighty Shadowfax, beats off the assault of the dread Nazgûl with a blast of radiant light. The legions of Mordor are broken and they scatter, but the defenders of Gondor have suffered terrible losses and have little hope remaining. And still Rohan does not come.

Among the fallen lies Faramir, last surviving son of Denethor and only heir to the Stewardship. He fought magnificently but was struck down. They bear him, deeply and perhaps fatally wounded, into the safety of the city.

> The Prince Imrahil brought Faramir to the White Tower, and he said: "Your son has returned, lord, after great deeds," and he told all that he had seen. But Denethor rose and looked upon the face of his son and was silent. Then he bade them make a bed in the chamber and lay Faramir upon it and depart. But he himself went up alone into the secret room under the summit of the Tower; and many who looked up thither at that time saw a pale light that gleamed and flickered from the narrow windows for a while, and then flashed and went out. And when Denethor descended again he went to Faramir and sat beside him without speaking, but the face of the Lord was grey, more deathlike than his son's.

The siege continues. The only hope lies in the coming of Rohan. The Rohirrim are ancient allies of Gondor; they have fought side by side in many battles, these two peoples. But Rohan does not come, and soon it may be too late. Now Mordor brings mighty engines of war against the defenses of the city, catapults thunder, and fiery missiles rain down. An endless horde of dark warriors stream up against the riven walls, as if drawn from a bottomless source. Courage begins to give way to utter despair.

In the citadel, Denethor sits by the body of his dying son and takes no part in the defense of his realm. Command devolves upon Gandalf, who labors mightily with all his courage and wit; but it seems that all is lost. The first circle of the city is aflame. Men are fleeing from the walls and leaving them unmanned. And Denethor curses the messengers who bring him such word.

"Why do the fools fly? Better to burn sooner than late, for burn we must. Go back to your bonfire! And if I go now to my pyre. To my pyre! No tomb for Denethor and Faramir. No tomb! No long slow sleep of death embalmed. We will burn like heathen kings before ever a ship sailed hither from the West. The West has failed. Go back and burn!"

A great battering ram bursts the Gate of Gondor. It falls thunderously. Through the riven gap rides the Lord of the Nazgûl, a terrible and faceless thing. All flee his coming save Gandalf, who stands in his path and confronts him, commanding that he fall back. The Lord of the Nazgûl laughs.

"Old fool!" he said. "Old fool! This is my hour. Do you not know Death when you see it? Die now and curse in vain!" And with that he lifted high his sword and flames ran down the blade.

Gandalf did not move. And in that very moment, away behind in some courtyard of the City, a cock crowed. Shrill and clear he crowed, recking nothing of wizardry and war, welcoming only the morning that in the sky far above the shadows of death was coming with the dawn.

And as if in answer there came from far away another

note. Horns, horns, horns. In dark Mindolluin's sides they
dimly echoed. Great horns of the North wildly blowing.
Rohan had come at last.

On the field of Pelennor the hosts of Rohan sweep
up against the hordes of Mordor. In the forefront rides
Théoden King, like some great warrior of ancient legend. His is the first sword to strike, his the hand that
hews down the black and scarlet banner of the Dark
Lord. From the Gates, where he confronts Gandalf the
White, the Lord of the Nazgûl cries out and vanishes.
Then, mounted between the foul wings of his hideous
flying steed, he hurtles against the Rohirrim the terror
of the Nazgûl. The old King of the Mark falls before
his wrath. But one knight of Rohan stands by the
fallen king to challenge the grim might of the Nazgûl's
Lord—a young knight named Dernhelm, who now
stands revealed as Théoden's daughter, Éowyn, who
has pretended to be a youth so as to fight beside her
father.

The princess-knight slays the great flying monster,
but the Lord of the Nazgûl, the Black Captain of the
hordes of Mordor, strikes her down and shatters her
shield with one great blow that breaks her arm. Then
he staggers under the chill bite of an unexpected blow.
It is the young Hobbit, Merry, who has ridden all the
long road from Rohan behind "Dernhelm" and whose
sword has injured the Black Captain in the moment of
his victory. The Lord of the Nazgûl reels as his guard
drops. At that moment Éowyn strikes from the ground.
Her sword cleaves him to death. His grim sword falls
and shatters. He crashes to the ground, and there is
nothing left of him but an empty helm and hauberk!
The ghostly thing which had donned these pieces of
war gear is fled, returning to the shadowy realm of

death from which the mighty will of the Lord of the Rings had summoned him.

Now young Éomer rides up to report victory. He is hailed by the dying Théoden as King of the Mark. The sorrowing victors bear the body of the fallen Théoden from the field. Gothmog, lieutenant of Mordor, seizes command of the broken forces of the Dark Lord, and the battle goes on. It is long and fierce, and toward the end of it even the gallant young king, Éomer, begins to lose heart. But then down the river the approach of a great fleet is seen. The knights waver, crying that the savage Corsairs of Umbar have come to swell the ranks of Mordor.

All seems lost. Éomer rides to the top of a hill and looks upon the host of dark ships, and feels the bitterness of defeat. He sings:

> Out of doubt, out of dark to the day's rising
> I came singing in the sun, sword unsheathing.
> To hope's end I rode and to heart's breaking:
> Now for wrath, now for ruin and a red nightfall!

But the tide has turned. Even as he gazes upon them and shakes his sword at the black ships, wonder and joy seize him. For from the foremost vessel a great standard unrolls upon the wind. A White Tree is emblazoned thereupon, and Seven Stars, and the sigil of Elendil above all—symbols no lord of Middle-earth had borne on the field of battle for years beyond counting.

Thus to the defense of Gondor comes Aragorn the son of Arathorn, Isildur's Heir, with Gimli and Legolas at his side and a host of his people, the Dúnedain, the Rangers of the North. The weary, half-defeated defenders feel their hearts swell with this unexpected coming of help.

> And the mirth of the Rohirrim was a torrent of laughter and a flashing of swords, and the joy and wonder of the city was a music of trumpets and a ringing of bells. But the hosts of Mordor were seized with bewilderment, and a great wizardry it seemed to them that their own ships should be filled with their foes; and a black dread fell on them, knowing that the tides of fate had turned against them and their doom was at hand.

The hosts of Éomer and of Aragorn cleave through the foe, and they meet to clasp hands amid the battle.

And the day is theirs.

But Denethor—they fear for him. Broken by what he supposes to be the loss of Faramir (who, although dying, is not yet dead), Denethor is sunken in a dark nightmare whereinto the light of reason and fact cannot penetrate. The funeral pyre is lit. His son lies upon it. Gandalf pushes past the maddened Steward and pulls the youth from the flames. Though raving with fever, Faramir yet lives. Denethor hurls himself on the pyre and meets his doom.

Soon Gandalf discovers the cause of Denethor's derangement. The Steward had possessed another *palantir,* for here as in Orthanc one of the stones-of-seeing was preserved. Denethor must have used it on that dark night when passers-by saw strange lights flickering from the windows of the secret room. The Dark Lord must have worked through the magic crystal to undermine Denethor's reason, as a means to weaken Gondor. Gandalf brings Faramir to the house of healing where Merry and the injured Éowyn lie. They despair of saving the young Steward; only a legendary remedy called the King's Touch can save him now. At

Gandalf's behest, Aragorn secretly enters the city and lays his healing hand and certain herbs on Faramir. He rests easily thereafter and his fever eases. And word runs through the City: the King has come again.

When all are rested and weapons honed and mail repaired, all the hosts of the West gather on the field of Pelennor and ride for the Black Gate to challenge the might of Mordor. The embassy of Sauron emerges from the grim portal in answer to their challenge and mocks them with the word that Frodo is taken. Gandalf will not surrender even to save the Ring bearer.

The scene shifts to the borders of Mordor. Sam, now the bearer of the Ring, which he has taken from Frodo's body, enters the Orc fortress under the Ring's invisibility spell and finds that Frodo lives. He had only been paralyzed by the numbing venom of Shelob's bite and has since recovered. They make their escape from the fortress in the confusion caused by Sam's unexpected appearance, armed with Elvish weapons, within the enemy stronghold. They struggle on through harsh desert land. They are not molested. After a frightful ordeal and terrible sufferings from thirst and exhaustion, they come at last to Mount Doom, where the Ring was originally forged. They are near the end of a long journey.

Frodo is deeply marked and ravaged by his burden now, weary and tainted with the sinister fascination that surrounds the Ring. They ascend to the brink of the chasm, where the crimson glow that seeps from the Crack of Doom itself beats around them. Then Frodo seems to freeze, as if unable to rid himself of the Thing he has borne for so long. Sam yells at him to go ahead and throw it in the fires. But Frodo refuses. In a sharp clear voice he says, "I do not choose now to do what I

came to do. I will not do this deed. *The Ring is mine!"*
Then

> Something struck Sam violently in the back, his legs
> were knocked from under him and he was flung aside,
> striking his head against the stony floor, as a dark shape
> sprang over him. . . .
> Sam got up. He was dazed, and blood streaming from
> his head dripped in his eyes. He groped forward, and then
> he saw a strange and terrible thing. Gollum on the edge
> of the abyss was fighting like a mad thing with an unseen
> foe. To and fro he swayed, now so near the brink that
> almost he tumbled in, now dragging back, falling to the
> ground, rising, and falling again. And all the while he
> hissed but spoke no words.
> The fires below awoke in anger, the red light blazed,
> and all the cavern was filled with a great glare and heat.
> Suddenly Sam saw Gollum's long hands draw upwards to
> his mouth; his white fangs gleamed, and then snapped as
> they bit. Frodo gave a cry, and there he was, fallen upon
> his knees at the chasm's edge. But Gollum, dancing like a
> mad thing, held aloft the ring, a finger still thrust within
> its circle. It shone now as if verily it was wrought of liv-
> ing fire.
> "Precious, precious, precious!" Gollum cried. "My Pre-
> cious! O my Precious!" And with that even as his eyes
> were lifted up to gloat on his prize, he stepped too far,
> toppled, wavered for a moment on the brink, and then
> with a shriek he fell. Out of the depths came his last wail
> *precious,* and he was gone.

Frodo, weakening at the last moment, had been unable to resist the lure of the Ring; but Gollum, following on his trail, attacked him and bit off Frodo's finger,
Ring and all. Now he and the Ring have vanished into
the fires of Mount Doom.

The mountain roars. Flames shoot up. Sam lifts up
the injured, shaken Frodo and helps him outside into
the air. Mordor shakes and quakes around them with
thunders. Towers fall and mountains crumble. The
Ring, the One Ring, the great Ring of Power is de-

stroyed: and with it, the greater part of Sauron's power is lost. Exhausted, shaken, drained to the limits of their strength and courage, Frodo and Sam have passed through countless perils to the completion of the task laid upon them back in far-off Rivendel.

On the Field of Cormallen, the Captains of the West are locked in a terrific battle with the iron hordes of Mordor. At the last moment the earth rocks beneath them, and high above the mountains a vast soaring blackness rises up into the sky, flickering with fire. The hills groan and shudder, and the Towers of the Gate collapse in rubble.

Gandalf cries out that the realm of Sauron has ended and that the Ring bearer has fulfilled the Quest.

And as the Captains gazed south to the Land of Mordor, it seemed to them that, black against the pall of cloud, there rose a huge shape of shadow, impenetrable, lightning-crowned, filling all the sky. Enormous it reared above the world, and stretched out towards them a vast threatening hand, terrible but impotent: for even as it leaned over them, a great wind took it, and it was all blown away, and passed; and then a hush fell.

The Captains bowed their heads; and when they looked up again, behold! their enemies were flying and the power of Mordor was scattering like dust in the wind.

Gandalf mounts the great eagle, Gwaihir, and flies over Mordor to snatch the bone-weary Hobbits from the fires of the riven mountain. They are swept up into the cold air and know no more until they awaken in the cool fragrance of Ithilien in Gondor. Still clad in the tattered clothes they had journeyed in, they are ushered into the presence of a great company. Dazzled, they blink as tall knights in glittering mail bow humbly before them. As trumpets sound, they pass to a tall throne set amid a mighty host, and thereupon

Aragorn the King greets them with great honor, and a minstrel of Gondor sings a lay of their deeds.

For a time they rest amid merriment and ease and heal their hurts. Faramir, now the Last Steward of Gondor, has recovered his strength and has come to love the valiant shield maiden, Éowyn of Rohan, daughter of the late Théoden. And in pageantry and splendor Aragorn enters his kingdom and is crowned King. Great personages come to visit the new monarch, among them the Lady Galadriel and Celeborn, and from afar come Master Elrond and Arwen his daughter, who is wed on midsummer day to the new King of Gondor.

At length the comrades part, venturing each to his home. Frodo, Sam, and Merry make a leisurely journey home, revisiting many of the places they had passed through earlier. They find terrible changes that have been wrought since they left many months before. The Shire has become a dismal place. Churlish ruffians and thieving renegades have seized power in the Shire, but the gallant heroes of the Quest have faced and fought with Trolls and Orcs and are not to be cowed by braggarts and bullies. The Scouring of the Shire is swift and thorough, and the Hobbits are alarmed to discover, at the end, that the secret master of the ruined Shire is none other than Saruman, the deposed magician of Orthanc. His magical powers have been stripped from him, but he has lost nothing of his cunning and malice. Frodo drives him forth, together with his whimpering slave, Grima Wormtongue. In a sudden burst of frenzied hate, taunted beyond endurance by his cruel master, Wormtongue surprisingly turns on Saruman and knifes him in the back. Frodo pities the tormented little man, but before he has time to halt his vengeful comrades, bows twang and Wormtongue falls dead.

Then follows the long, melancholy task of cleaning up the Shire and restoring it to peace and plenty and assisting its downtrodden inhabitants to recover their self-respect. This is a wearisome and heartbreaking task, but finally it is finished. Sam marries his village sweetheart, and the days drift on in a lazy, summery way. But all is not done.

Frodo has taken a lasting inward hurt from the long agony of bearing the poisonous talisman of evil magic. He becomes ill from time to time and slowly wastes from his wound. He knows he can never be completely healed, at least not here in Middle-earth. But Arwen, the daughter of Elrond Half-elven, who is now Queen in Gondor, has relinquished her place in the Blessed Realm to him, choosing to stay in Middle-earth rather than to return to the ancient land of the Elves oversea (for the elves are withdrawing from the World of Men, now that the Third Age is ended). Frodo knows that in that holy place of utter peace he can truly be healed. He therefore sets forth on one more journey, to the Grey Havens, where the Elven-folk take ship for their far-off land beyond the sea. With him go Elrond and Galadriel and others, riding for the sea. At the Havens they meet Gandalf, whose task in Middle-earth is also done. Last farewells are made. Frodo and old Bilbo and Gandalf bid Sam farewell and depart. And Sam returns to the Shire and to his family.

And the sails were drawn up, and the wind blew, and slowly the ship slipped away down the long grey firth; and the light of the glass of Galadriel that Frodo bore glimmered and was lost. And the ship went out into the High Sea and passed on into the West, until at last on a night of rain Frodo smelled a sweet fragrance on the air and heard the sound of singing that came over the water. And then it seemed to him that as in his dream in the house of Bombadil, the grey rain-curtain turned all to silver glass and was rolled back, and he beheld white shores and beyond them a far green country under a swift sunrise.

And it is here that the long story ends.

8.
The Trilogy—
Satire or Allegory?

> The realm of fairy-story is wide and deep and
> high and filled with many things; all manner of
> beasts and birds are found there; shoreless seas
> and stars uncounted; beauty that is an enchant-
> ment, and an ever-present peril; both joy and
> sorrow as sharp as swords. In that realm a man
> may, perhaps, count himself fortunate to have
> wandered, but its very richness and strangeness
> tie the tongue of a traveller who would report
> them. And while he is there it is dangerous for
> him to ask too many questions, lest the gates
> should be shut and the keys be lost.
> J. R. R. TOLKIEN, *On Fairy-Stories*

So much for the actual narrative content of what the
Boston *Herald-Traveler* has called "one of the best
wonder-tales ever written—and one of the best-writ-
ten," and which W. H. Auden has hailed as "a masterpiece of its genre." I have devoted so much space in
the foregoing chapters to a summary of the trilogy's
plot because, from this point on, we will be exploring
the text in considerable detail to search out its literary
ancestors, to ascertain the precise tradition to which it
belongs, and to discuss some of the curiosities of the
story. But let me emphasize again that merely reading
the summary in the previous few chapters is certainly
no substitute for reading the trilogy itself. I have
quoted from the actual text on occasion; but Professor
Tolkien's prose must be experienced at first-hand for
an appreciation of its full flavor and the music of his
writing.

Mr. Auden's comment raises the question: to exactly which genre does *LOTR* belong? Accepting, as I do, Mr. Auden's opinion that Tolkien "has succeeded more completely than any other previous writer in this genre," we are still left with the task of identifying and classifying the genre of the trilogy.

To settle this question is fully within the scope and purpose of this book; in fact, finding an appropriate classification for the trilogy is badly needed. A very large number of the Professor's most enthusiastic admirers appear to be new to reading (irrespective of age, since the appeal of *LOTR* runs up and down the whole spectrum of the human condition) and seem to hold the erroneous opinion that *The Lord of the Rings* is unique and unprecedented in modern literature. In fact, even some of the reviewers and critics who were quoted earlier appear to believe that nothing whatsoever has been written in this field and at this level of artistry since the Good Old Days of Spenser, Ariosto, and company. This is simply not true.

The Lord of the Rings has most often, I would say, been compared to Spenser. That is, to Spenser's masterpiece, a very long poem called *The Faerie Queene,* which is both a poetic romance and an allegory. But the trilogy is not in any way either a satire or an allegory, but a romance pure and simple. Equating Tolkien with the great masters of allegorical romance is an easy and logical notion because there are certain points of similarity in depth and richness and complexity of style and background detail; but these are superficial. Tolkien is merely telling a story, and it has no overtones of symbolic meaning at all.

LOTR is, quite simply, a fantasy novel. Now fantasy, as such, is a branch of fiction very much in disrepute these days, although at one time it was a respected and legitimate area for the fine art of storytelling. Rare was the literary artist, or even the hack, who did not exploit its numerous possibilities, without discriminating against "make-believe." Quite a case could, as a matter of fact, be made for the fantasy tale as one of the major areas in world literature, for few of the most highly regarded names in English or Continental letters avoided it. Rabelais, Chaucer, Goethe, Milton, Cervantes, Swift, Shakespeare,* Voltaire, Byron, Ariosto, Keats, Flaubert, Spenser, Dante, Marlowe, and even a Brontë or two wrote fantasies—to say nothing of Stevenson, Kipling, Doyle, Wilde, Haggard, and Anatole France.

However (it may be argued), since Swift, Cervantes, Spenser, and Bunyan wrote fantasies that were also allegories or satires, why could not *LOTR* be considered as such? Superficially, some sort of case for Tolkien's trilogy being allegorical could be made out; surely it presents the War Between Good and Evil (or Light and Darkness) when the plot is reduced to the very simplest of terms. Some readers have even found in the struggle between the forces of the West and eastern Mordor an allegory of the cold war between the democracies of Western Europe and totalitarian Russia—with the all-important, incredibly dangerous Ring as a symbol for today's nuclear weaponry. But then, any action yarn about the Good Guys versus the

---

* Without straining credibility, it could be said that *Hamlet* is a ghost story (since the specter of Hamlet's father provides the prince's motive and sets the play in action); *Macbeth,* with its witches and grisly phantom of Banquo at the feast, has elements of the horror story, and both *The Tempest* and *A Midsummer Night's Dream,* considered from the standpoint of plot alone, are simply fairy tales.

Bad Guys, such as a Max Brand Western, is capable of similar interpretation, thus reducing the argument to nonsense. The significant element would be the author's stated intention. Spenser's *Faerie Queene* is avowedly a satire on the political figures of Elizabethan Britain, combined with an allegory of the triumph of virtue over vice. The political interpretation is almost lost to any but the most scholarly specialist, deeply learned in the trivial minutiae of Elizabethan politics. The moral meanings, however, are blatantly obvious—Spenser literally rubs the readers' noses in them.

As originally planned, *The Faerie Queene* was divided into twelve adventures.* Each adventure celebrates the victorious struggle of one of Aristotle's classic Twelve Virtues—Holiness, Temperance, Courtesy, Justice, et al.—over a corresponding vice.

The symbolism is worked out in the characters of the poem. For example, Holiness is represented by the Red Crosse Knight, who is also supposed to be Saint George; Sir Calidore stands for Courtesy; Sir Guyon represents Temperance; and so on. The overall hero of the poem is Prince Arthur, who has not yet become King Arthur. He is supposed to represent a conglomeration of all twelve Virtues wrapped up in a single heroic package.

---

* Like most epic poems written since the decline of classical literature (and some literary historians consider *The Faerie Queene* to be a legitimate English epic, although it is not), Spenser's poem is incomplete. It was not abandoned or left unfinished for any reason—as was the fate of Keats' *Hyperion,* Byron's *Don Juan,* or many another recent attempt at the epic—but (so the story goes) is extant only in part, the last half having been destroyed in a fire. Even in fragmentary form, it is among the longest poems in the language.

So much for the allegorical meanings, which are clearly stated in the text of the poem. The second level of symbolism, the identification of each Virtue character with a contemporary figure in the political life of the era, is far less obvious. Sir Artegall stands for a certain Lord Grey de Wilton; Sir Calidore (Courtesy) is supposed to be the courtier-poet Sir Philip Sidney, in real life Spenser's patron and friend; and so on. The Faerie Queene of the title is Gloriana, who stands for Queen Elizabeth I herself, to whom Spenser dedicated the poem. And that paragon of all Virtues, Prince Arthur, may perhaps have been intended for the Earl of Leicester, as John Hayward has suggested.*

The whole point of such an elaborate and highly complicated gallimaufry of symbolism adds up to a total waste of time on the author's part if the reader is unable to get that point. This is what happened to Spenser; even back in his own Elizabethan time, such contemporary readers as Sir Walter Raleigh found themselves unable to piece out the meaning of the "allegorical Devises" Spenser used and to make out the hidden references so "cloudily enwrapped." Sir Walter, having waded laboriously through the first three books of the work, was forced to ask the poet for a detailed explanation, saying (in effect), "Very pretty, but what

---

* In his introduction to the Heritage Press edition, published to commemorate the coronation of Queen Elizabeth II. *The Faerie Queene,* I must add, is certainly one of those "classics" which very few persons today can read for pleasure. I plodded through the whole thing myself, but it took me a solid year to do it, and at times I had to flog myself back to the task. This is partly because of the extreme complexity of Spenser's narrative, and partly because of the deliberate archaisms he employed—archaic even for 1580: words like "whyleare," "ypight," "agraste," "noriture," "algates," and so on.

the hell does it all *mean?*" To which Spenser replied in a letter dated January 23, 1589, in which he explained the general aim and scope of the poem. "The generall end of all the booke," he wrote to Sir Walter Raleigh, "is to fashion a gentleman or noble person in vertuous and gentle discipline."

The Faerie Queene has its admirers, notably Shelley, Keats, Byron, and, more recently, T. S. Eliot and C. S. Lewis. Nevertheless, Spenser's problems lay in the fact that, even in his own time, the allegorical interpretation of life and conduct had already become pretty old-fashioned, and *The Faerie Queene* was just about the last gasp of this school of writing, which had long since had its day and was vanishing from the literary scene.*

If Professor Tolkien had any such political or moral layers of symbolism in mind when composing *The Lord of the Rings,* he has been extraordinarily successful in concealing them from even the most astute and exhaustive of his many readers, such as, perhaps, the lady who lost count after having read the entire trilogy thirty times over.

In fact, the Professor is often questioned on precisely this point by interviewers. He has gone on record with very emphatic denials that *The Lord of the Rings* is "about anything but itself." In one place he quite firmly states, "It has *no* allegorical intentions, general, particular or topical, moral, religious or political."

---

* Although John Bunyan was to attempt a revival of the method, in much simpler and easier-to-read form, in his prose romance, *The Pilgrim's Progress,* he did not have much success, either, except for a flurry in the late nineteenth century which could hardly have been due to intrinsic interest or literary quality.

And in his new foreword (I, xi) to the Ballantine edition of the trilogy, he goes even further in discussing his full intentions:

> I cordially dislike allegory in all its manifestations, and always have done so since I grew old and wary enough to detect its presence. *I much prefer history, true or feigned,* with its varied applicability to the thought and experience of readers. I think that many confuse "applicability" with "allegory"; but the one resides in the freedom of the reader, and the other in the purposed domination of the author.
>
> An author cannot of course remain wholly unaffected by his experience, but the ways in which a story-germ uses the soil of experience are extremely complex, and attempts to define the process are at best guesses from evidence that is inadequate and ambiguous. [Italics added.]

Specifically countering the apparent political symbolism of the trilogy (i.e. the similarity which some readers or critics have noticed between the war of Gondor against Mordor and the current cold-war East-West confrontation), Tolkien further stated, while discussing some of his readers who, inferring a correlation between the Scouring of the Shire in the third volume and political conditions in modern Britain, presumed that the one reflected something of the other: "It does not. It is an essential part of the plot . . . without, need I say, any allegorical significance *or contemporary political reference whatsoever*" (italics added).

Just in case some readers are not yet fully convinced and a further defense is needed against the satire-cum-allegory interpretation of the trilogy beyond the flat and frequent denials by the author himself, let me quote from one of the letters of C. S. Lewis, which has a bearing on this topic, before passing along to more fruitful areas of exploration.

In a letter to Fr. Peter Milward, dated September 22, 1956, C. S. Lewis wrote:

> Tolkien's book is not an allegory—a form he dislikes. You'll get nearest to his mind on such subjects by studying his essay on Fairy Tales in the *Essays Presented to Charles Williams*. His root idea of narrative art is "sub-creation"—the making of a secondary world. What you wd. call "a pleasant story for the children" wd. be to him *more serious* than an allegory. But for *his* views read the essay, which is indispensable.

Having concluded that *The Lord of the Rings* is neither satire nor allegory let us turn to Professor Tolkien's essay and examine his thinking on "sub-creation" to see if it gives any insight into the nature and genre of *The Lord of the Rings*.

9.

Tolkien's Theory
of the Fairy Story

> FAIRY TALE. 1. a story about fairies. 2 a state-
> ment or account of something imaginary or in-
> credible.
>
> *The American College Dictionary*

The essay to which C. S. Lewis referred in his letter quoted in the last chapter was first composed as an Andrew Lang Lecture. Professor Tolkien notes (in *Tree and Leaf*) that "On Fairy-Stories" was delivered in somewhat shorter form as a lecture at the University of St. Andrews in 1938. It was later slightly enlarged and printed in a volume of essays in honor of Charles Williams published by Oxford University Press in 1947. Seventeen years later, with a few minor alterations, it was again reprinted (together with a short story called "Leaf by Niggle" from the *Dublin Review*) in the book *Tree and Leaf,* which George Allen and Unwin, Tolkien's British publishers, issued in 1964. The American edition was published in 1965 by Houghton Mifflin.

To these last two editions, Tolkien contributed a new introductory note. In it he observes that the essay "may still be found interesting, especially by those to whom *The Lord of the Rings* has given pleasure," because the essay was originally written "in the same period (1938-39) when *The Lord of the Rings* was beginning to unroll itself and to unfold prospects of labour and exploration in yet unknown country as daunting to me as to the hobbits."

The essay does indeed afford us a valuable glimpse into the mind (and especially into the creative philosophy) of the author during the actual writing of his book. As such, it richly deserves a close look, as C. S. Lewis wisely suggested in his letter to Fr. Milward.

Early in the essay Tolkien establishes the point that most so-called fairy stories do not in fact have any fairies in their cast of characters. The average reader of fairy stories, if required to name typical examples of the genre, would be likely to list something like "Puss-in-Boots" or "Little Red Riding Hood"—fairy stories noteworthy for the total and complete absence of any fairies in their pages. The Professor continues in this vein, to suggest that most (though not all) of what we call fairy stories are not actually so much about fairies as they are about the universe of Faerie itself. He puts it this way: "Most good 'fairy-stories' are about the *adventures* of men in the Perilous Realm or upon its shadowy marches." This fairly self-evident thought brings to mind the obvious point that Tolkien himself would doubtless define *LOTR* as a legitimate fairy story, albeit one of inordinate length.

He goes on to present the argument that the marvels and fantastic elements in a valid fairy story must be true. That is, the author cannot take refuge in the plot-device of "it was all a dream" *—neither can the magics and miracles of the tale turn out to have been stage illusions or hallucinations. It is essential, he states, that the genuine fairy story should be presented as true.

Side-stepping as irrelevant the fascinating issue of the origins of the fairy story or of the fairies themselves, he continues to a deeper consideration of the *matter* of Faerie. He delves into the connections among fairy stories, mythology, and religion; and, briefly, into the connections between history and mythology, drawing the interesting conclusion that history often resembles myth or legend because both are ultimately formed from the same stuff.

Then follows an examination of the old idea that fairy stories are mostly for children—a concept with which, I am sure, every fantasy reader would disagree as heartily as myself. Happily, the Professor demolishes this noisome concept and explains the relegation of the fairy story to the nursery as merely an accident in our domestic history. He points out, moreover, that the very concept itself has become deleterious to the production of good fairy literature. The teller (or reteller) of such tales has himself come to consider children as his natural audience. This enables him to push off on the helpless child a mountain of second-rate writing, because the writers may count on the credulity of the juvenile mind—the child's inclination to believe completely in what the written page tells him.

Coleridge called this state of mind the "willing sus-

---

* Which would, of course, render invalid any claims on the part of *Alice* to being a fairy story. It would have to find its place, then, among general fantasy or some such subspecies as dream literature.

pension of disbelief"; it is absolutely vital to the reader's enjoyment of any work of fantastic art, whether it be poem, story, or whatever. Tolkien, however, rejects this point about the child-reader's credulity and insists on higher standards in the making of fantasies. The writer's skill in making his fabricated world complete and realistic and self-consistent in every last detail is the more important element in a genuine (and successful) fairy story or fantasy.

As he puts it: "What really happens is that the story-maker proves a successful 'sub-creator' " in a successful fairy story. "He makes a Secondary World which your mind can enter. Inside it, what he relates is 'true': it accords with the laws of that world."

Next the Professor turns to this theory of subcreation. It is, he believes, not essentially the domain of the fairy story as such at all but is the universe of all art. All artists are involved in the making of Secondary Worlds. The worlds must be self-consistent and in agreement with their own natural laws, even though these laws may frequently be at enormous variance with those of our own world, in which we live our daily lives. Subcreation—the building of sound and solid Secondary Worlds—as Tolkien sees it, is the goal of all art. And it is best achieved through the medium of the fantasy tale.

Fantasy aspires to the elvish art of enchantment, he holds; and a truly successful work of fantasy more nearly approaches true Enchantment than all other forms of art.*

---

* Fantasy becomes unsuccessful, Tolkien implies, when it either fails to observe its own basic laws or fails to take itself seriously enough. He illustrates this with a reference to Andrew Lang's two Pantouflian romances, *Prince Prigio* and *Prince Ricardo*. Tolkien characterizes them as either patronizing or (deadliest of all) covertly

He goes on to discuss the value and importance of fantasy—that it serves to reintroduce us to the wonders and beauties of the natural world around us, which we tend to accept rather than to wonder at as legitimate Things of Marvel. He also turns to the materials from which fantasy is made—materials which lie all around us—showing how fantasy enlarges and underscores our appreciation of the real world, the Primary World.

> Fantasy is made out of the Primary World, but a good craftsman loves his material, and has a knowledge and feeling for clay, stone and wood which only the art of making can give. By the forging of Gram cold iron was revealed; by the making of Pegasus horses were ennobled; in the Trees of the Sun and Moon root and stock, flower and fruit are manifested in glory.

The mark of true fantasy, the seal of authenticity upon it, by which it may be differentiated from the bogus and the imitation, is the quality of "joy": the joy of the maker in the thing that he has made, when it is well-made; the joy of the reader who has fallen under the spell of the subcreator and dwells for a little time within a Secondary World which is made lovingly and with care.

This quality of "joy" is largely dependent upon the inner consistency of the story. "Every writer making a secondary world . . . hopes that the peculiar quality of this secondary world (if not all the details) are derived from Reality, or are flowing into it."

---

sniggering, with an eye on the other grown-ups present. He writes: "I will not accuse Andrew Lang of sniggering, but certainly he smiled to himself, and certainly too often he had an eye on the faces of other clever people over the heads of his child-audience—to the very grave detriment of the *Chronicles of Pantouflia*."

Reality, inner consistency, "true"—how can these elements or characteristics be placed in juxtaposition with fantasy, which we usually think of as being formed largely from unreality? "The peculiar quality of the 'joy' in successful fantasy can thus be explained as a sudden glimpse of the underlying reality or truth."

If this essay truly reflects Professor Tolkien's philosophy as a fantasy writer, perhaps we can begin to understand something of the inner nature of his work. Obviously the definitions of *LOTR* as either satire or allegory must be rejected. The work has no hidden meaning; it is nothing more than a fantasy novel, a story, a made thing, a fairy story in Tolkien's unique definition of that term.

How well, then, does his own trilogy match his stated requirements for a successful fantasy? For one thing, keeping in mind his thesis that a fantasy "must be presented as *true*," we can see how he has lived up to this criterion. *The Lord of the Rings* is presented as a true history, and the author has buttressed his contention by surrounding the tale with an elaborate machinery of appendices, containing factual data on his world not given in the narrative. His Middle-earth languages are equipped with copious vocabularies and alphabets. He has worked out a chronology of the previous ages which gives a historical summary, complete with dates, for many centuries. Lists of kings and genealogies support the major characters of his story and supply background history.

This, of course, is completely in line with his belief that the subcreator of a Secondary World must make his fabricated cosmos complete, realistic, and self-consistent in every detail. He neither writes for children nor counts much on the "willing suspension of disbelief" to make his narrative and its world credible. The one element most readers of Tolkien find most fascinating is the air of conviction and authority that runs through every page: to the reader, Middle-earth is a real and whole and genuine place.

What about his final contention—that the vital quality he calls "joy" should be present through sudden glimpses of underlying truth? It is a little difficult to make out quite what he means, but I have arrived at a satisfactory interpretation—at least for myself. I do not think the Professor is talking about linking up his Secondary World to the genuine texture of Northern myth and trying to convince us that his world is our own at a period before formal history was recorded. Although he uses Dwarves and Elves and Trolls and Dragons, all stock figures from Norse or Germanic literature, I doubt that such was his purpose. By underlying realities he probably alludes to the eternal verities of human nature. While the trilogy is, on the surface at least, an entertaining narrative of fantastic adventure, the moral element is plainly obvious. The jealous, the greedy, the proud, the power-hungry, all receive commensurate punishments. The humble, the unselfish, the hard-working, the honest, and the noble are rewarded beyond their own estimates of their due. Boromir dies, not because he was wicked, but because his ambition and pride grew so strong as to conquer his innate nobility.

Perhaps it is rather old-fashioned, the idea of literature as teaching a moral, but if so, much of the greatest literature of all ages must be called old-fashioned.

With the above points in mind, then, we can see that the so-called eccentricities in the trilogy—the elaborate critical machinery of alphabets, linguistic supplements, genealogies, and historical summaries—are not just the outgrowth of a don's scholarly hobbies, but are fully required by the author's own definition of a true and valid work of fantasy.

Or, as he calls it, a fairy story. But Tolkien goes far beyond anything the dictionary would give in broadening the traditional meaning of the term. He has broadened it to include the entire world of art.

This point raises another question. If *The Lord of the Rings* is a fantasy novel, another problem in definition arises. For the term "fantasy" is itself capable of very wide application. What kind of a fantasy is the Tolkien trilogy? Does it belong to the whimsy of James Stephens' *The Crock of Gold* or to the supernatural horror of H. P. Lovecraft's *Weird Shadow Over Innsmouth*? To the swashbuckling heroics of Robert E. Howard's "Conan" stories or the ironic symbolism of James Branch Cabell's *Jurgen*? To the high adventure of H. Rider Haggard's *She* or to the subtle legendry of Lord Dunsany's *Idle Days on the Yann*? To the dream narrative of George Macdonald's *Phantastes* or to the mythopoeism of modern "historical" novels laid in the times of King Arthur or Greek myth, such as Robert Graves' *Hercules, My Shipmate*?

For fantasy is a catch-all term that encompasses everything from Homer and Swift and Kafka to Poe, Milton, and *The Turn of the Screw*. Science fiction is a part of fantasy; so is the literature of gothic horror and even children's books like L. Frank Baum's American masterpiece, *The Wonderful Wizard of Oz* and its forty-odd sequels. Any genre so broad as to include both *Dracula* and *Utopia* demands further redefining.

The trilogy is most obviously cognate with epic poetry. It is truly Homeric in size, in concept, in the sweep and grandeur of the narrative, in the fact that the heroes are painted larger than life. Thus it would be no misnomer to class *LOTR* as "epic fantasy." In point of fact, such a genre does exist, and its roots may be traced all the way back to the epic literature of the Greeks and the Romans. But this definition is not quite sufficient. Tolkien draws from other bodies of literature as well as the tradition of the classical epic. He has absorbed much of the tradition and form of the Norse saga, much from Germanic folktale and legend, much from medieval romance, Grail quest, and heroic tale, and to a certain extent from other fantasy novelists.

To completely understand the form and themes of *The Lord of the Rings,* to see it "in the round," so to speak, as an epic fantasy, we must trace these traditions back to their roots and see how the concept grew and developed to result in the school of the epic fantasy novel to which Tolkien so clearly belongs

10.

Fantasy in the Classical Epic

The kings that fought for Helen
Are gone like wraiths away,
And all their wars are done now
And all their lusts, for aye;
But he that harped of Helen,
His fingers strike and strum,
Though Helen's hands are dust now
And Helen's lips are dumb.

J. U. NICOLSON, *Song*

There are two major themes in *The Lord of the Rings:* the theme of the war between the Captains of the West against the sinister might of Sauron, and the theme of the quest of a small company of heroes to bear the dreadful talisman of Sauron's power to the place where it may be destroyed. In Tolkien's work these two plot strands are expertly interwoven.

In the literature of the classical epic the dual themes of War and Quest are generally kept quite separate, although few epics were written that did not use one or the other of them. This can be seen most clearly in the works of Homer, himself the originator of the epic tradition. His *Iliad* is about the Trojan War, while the *Odyssey* is concerned with the wanderings and adventures of a hero in quest of his home. Our own quest to find the source of *The Lord of the Rings* takes us first to the world Homer created and the world in which he lived.

THE WORLD OF THE EPIC

"Epic" has been defined as a long, serious poem in an elevated style, relating a series of heroic achievements or events. But the modern word comes from the Latin *epicus,* which in turn was derived from the Greek *epikos,* which had its ultimate origin in *epos,* "a speech, tale, or song."

The early practitioners of the epic had in mind something quite different from our modern use of the word. To them, an epic was something which was meant to be recited (not sung as a lyric poem was meant to be sung) and differing from the drama only in that it was delivered without any attempt at imitative action. Aristotle listed as the only essentials of epic a dignified theme, an inner organic unity, and the orderly progress of the action.

The era of the rise of epic literature in Greece took place somewhere around the eighth century before the Christian Era, and ended roughly around 650 B.C. In those days man was still involved in the world of his own imagination. By this I mean that very little had actually been discovered about the world, its place in the universe, or nature. Everything men saw around them was interpreted through their own imagination. It could truthfully be said that, in the beginning, man created the world. For, like a fantasy writer mapping out an invented worldscape, man built up his own picture of his world. It was flat as a tabletop. The sky came down covering it like an inverted bowl. The whole was surrounded by a river shaped like a serpent swallowing its own tail. The sun, moon, and stars were somehow affixed to the crystalline layers of the sky, and these layers turned within one another like those intricate Chinese globes whose interiors are painstakingly sculpted into a series of concentric circles.

Man shared his world with all manner of fantastic beings. There were the gods, of course, usually a round dozen or so, each with his own clearly limited area of responsibility, one being governor of the seas, another lord of the winds, and so on. Then there were races of semidivinities acting as intermediaries between man and god. Some were harmless nature spirits who inhabited trees, streams, and the like. Others, less substantial, dwelled in the elements of Earth, Air, Fire, and Water. Then there were ghosts. Some were of the opinion that these dwelled in one or another sort of shadowy underground region, but others said that they passed from mortal life as men to inhabit other living forms. Every beetle or begonia, to early man, might be inhabited by his great-grandmother or by a demon.

Then there were the beasts. The real world is bad enough, with its scorpions, cobras, sharks, and maneating tigers; but the inventive imagination of early societies went on to dream up imaginary horrors and ghastlier creatures to lurk in every shadowy grove or hollow hill. There was the dragon, for example, clad in adamantine scales and winged like a bat, ever ready to snort fire and brimstone at the drop of a knightly helm. Or the hybrids, such as the gryphon, made up of leftover parts of eagle, lion, and serpent; and the wyvern, the firedrake, the hydra, the hippogriff, the sphinx, and the basilisk—a small lizard so remarkably ugly that a good look at it could kill the viewer; and other creatures of similar kidney, nowadays met with most frequently on coats-of-arms. And in some remote corner of the world—around Java or Borneo, say—grew the fearsome Upas Tree, so poisonous that if a high-flying bird so much as touched it with its shadow, the feathered little fellow dropped dead as a stone. Of course none of these gods, ghosts, or gorgons had the slightest existence in reality, any more than this tabletop world resembled the real world of nature, but that never stopped anyone from adding to the supply of imaginative flora and fauna whenever he had a good idea. And whether or not any of it was true seemed somehow irrelevant.

Consider, for example, that serious old sober-sides, Pliny, as much of a pragmatist as any other ex-cavalry colonel. In his *Natural History,* Book VII, with perfect seriousness he describes the Cyclopes and the Laestrygones; the Arimaspi (a "people remarkable for having one eye in the centre of their forehead"), who wage continual war with the griffins; the inhabitants of Abarimon, "who have their feet turned backward behind their legs"; the Ophiogenes, whose bodies are so poisonous that if a snake bites them the snake dies; the Machlyes, who "perform the function of either sex alternately" and have the right breast of a female and the left of a male; the Thibii tribe of Pontus who have two pupils in one eye and the likeness of a horse in the other and who are invulnerable to drowning; and the Monocoli or Umbrella-foot tribe, who have only one leg and enormous feet ("in the hotter weather they lie on their backs . . . and protect themselves with the shadow of their feet"); to say nothing of the people to the west, who are doubly remarkable in that they have no necks at all and their eyes are situated in their shoulders; and a race among the Nomads of India called the Sciritae, who have nostrils like snakes.

THE EPIC

In such a world, it is not at all surprising that, when men invented writing and began putting down stories, his first literary ventures came out as fantasies.

When we think of epics, we tend to think of Greek epics—that is to say Homer. But there were epics before Homer—for example, *Gilgamesh*. This ancient epic, which has been called "the first great poem in the world," is at least a thousand years older than the *Odyssey* or the Vedic hymns or Akhenaton's *Hymn to the Sun* or the legends and lyrics in the Bible. We have it in a very late translation, found in the private library of the world's first collector of literature (on tablets), King Assur-bani-pal of Assyria (whom the Greeks, for some reason, called "Sardanapalus"). Assur-bani-pal reigned in the seventh century before Christ, but the poem dates back much farther than that—it probably originated somewhere on the far side of 2000 B.C., and it is a fantasy.

Gilgamesh, King of Uruk, comes from an unusual family. His father, for example, makes Methuselah a relative youngster—he reigned for 1,200 years. Gilgamesh is a superhero, like Hercules or Robert E. Howard's Conan, much given to fighting monsters and perilous journeys. He battles "the Humbaba," a ferocious giant with the face of a lion and the fangs of a dragon. Nevertheless, Gilgamesh makes mighty short work of him. In his various travels the hero crosses the dark waters of Kur the death river, a sort of Sumerian version of the Styx, and ventures into the Garden of the Gods, and so on. There are many other Sumerian, Babylonian, and Assyrian epics, all lost and buried long ago and rediscovered only in modern times.

Some few experts have argued that the Homeric poems bear some traces of Gilgamesh influence. The Greek epics began with Homer, so far as we know. If there were any epics before his time, they have not survived. This Homer (more correctly *Homeros*) is a baffling individual. Nobody knows where he was born, although various authorities find reasons to put forward Smyrna, Chios, Colophon, Salamis, Rhodos, Argos, and Athenae as his birthplace.* And nobody knows exactly when he flourished; estimates range from the rather reasonable birthdate of 685 B.C. (put forward by the historian Theopompus) to the wildly unlikely date of 1159 B.C. (Philostratus). The simple fact of the matter is that we cannot say for sure who Homer was, or when he was born. But there is believed to have been an authoritative Athenian text for the Homeric poems in the second half of the sixth century B.C. although in fact there is no absolute proof that Homer was solely responsible for the *Iliad* and the *Odyssey*.

As for the two epics, both are fantasies. The *Iliad* is concerned with the wars against Troy—or rather, with a single episode in that war: the misunderstanding that caused strife between King Agamemnon, the leader of the Achaean host, and Achilles, the greatest of the warriors under his command. In the tale the Olympian

---

* While others find perfectly good reasons to claim he was born in Kyme, Ithaca, Ios, Pylos, or Sparta. Even Egypt and Babylon have some claim on him.

gods bustle about manipulating history and snatching this or that favorite hero from the jaws of doom—the chief area of the fantasy element. In the *Odyssey* we have the story of how one of the heroes returned home after the war. In tracing the wanderings of Odysseus, Homer goes in for some spectacular imaginary geography and takes the reader on a guided tour of the magic islands of Calypso and Circe, the isle of the Lotus Eaters, and so on.

Both are great works of poetry, although very dissimilar. The *Iliad* is probably the first psychological novel in literature, while the *Odyssey* is straight swashbuckling heroics—in Ezra Pound's fine phrase, the "high-water mark for the adventure story."

Homer—whether he was one man or twenty—was a superlative writer of highly imaginative genius, and his epics made a tremendous impression on the poets who came after him. So strong was the impression, in fact, that many followed in his footsteps and composed more epics in his manner: poet after poet bent his attentions to those other parts of the gigantic Troy tale which Homer had left untouched. Poem after poem was attached to the Homerica, either before the twin epics or between them or after them. This practice went on for many centuries, until at last there existed a kind of gigantic encyclopedia in verse, a universal history made up of at least sixteen epics, which covered the entire history of the universe (as known to the Greeks) from the creation down to the marriage of Odysseus' two sons, Telegonus and Telemachus.

Of all this Epic Cycle, as it is called, we have today only the *Iliad* and the *Odyssey*. Save for Homer alone, time has laid a heavy hand on the works of the other cyclic poets. Outside a few comments on them by such ancient scholars as Proclus, a brief synopsis or so, an occasional line or two directly quoted, all these works are gone.*

The cyclic epics were composed in no particular order and by several different poets scattered across centuries. In Hellenistic times the cyclic poems were arranged in chronological order, apparently by Zenodotus of Ephesus, about the beginning of the third century B.C. The Alexandrian scholars arranged them in this order:

First came the *Titanomachia* (The War of the Titans), which is ascribed to either Eumelus of Corinth or Arctinus of Miletus. It told of the union of Heaven and Earth, how the Titans sprang from that union, and of the fabulous war. Two lines from it are preserved, and a half dozen references to its subject matter exist.

Then came three poems about the legendary history of Thebes. The first of these is the *Oidipodeia,* whose reputed author is Cinaethon. One single line survives from its original 6,600 verses. Second is the *Thebais,* which is sometimes ascribed to Homer, Antimachus, Colophon, or Claros. It tells the story of the Seven Against Thebes, and we have twenty-one lines from it. Third is the *Epigonoi,* whose authorship is assigned to Homer or Antimachus of Teos. It originally contained 7,000 verses, but only one line from it is extant today. We have a pretty good idea about the content of these three Theban epics because Sophocles followed their plots when he wrote his plays.

---

* To be precise, only 135 lines have been salvaged from the wreckage of time. All of these references and the scanty quotations are given in a volume published by Heinemann and edited by Hugh G. Evelyn-White under the title *Hesiod, the Homeric Hymns and Homerica.*

Then came the Trojan Cycle, beginning with the *Cypria* by Stasinus of Cyprus or Hegesias (or Hegesinus) of Salamis (or of Halicarnassus). Written in eleven books, it told how the Trojan War began—the golden apple, the Judgment of Paris, the stealing away of Helen, and so on, followed by the gathering of the Achaean host and the war, up to the beginning of the *Iliad*. About fifty-three lines survive, and the grammarian Proclus has left us a thousand-word outline of the plot; all together, then, we know more about the style, content, and substance of the *Cypria* than of any other Cyclic epic except the Homerica.

The *Iliad* follows the *Cypria,* and after it comes the *Aethiopis,* ascribed to the same Arctinus who is sometimes the reputed author of the *Titanomachia.* It contained five books and picked up the story right from the end of the *Iliad.* In the *Iliad* Patroclus and Hector and several other heroes were killed. Arctinus therefore brings in a new team—first Penthesileia the Amazon, daughter of Ares the god of war, and Memnon the king of Ethiopia, clad in armor made by the god Hephaestus, as well as several others. Arctinus lived about 776 B.C. Only two lines are still extant, but Proclus has a synopsis.

Next is the *Iliasmikra* (the "Little Iliad") of Lesches (or Lescheos) of Pyrrha (or Mitylene) who lived around 660 B.C. This one contains the last portion of the Troy tale—Odysseus' acquisition of the arms of Achilles, the building of the Trojan Horse, and how the Greeks ostensibly sailed away, leaving the Trojans to knock down their walls to let the giant horse in. Since the "new team" (the Amazon Penthesileia and the Ethiopian Memnon) were killed off by Arctinus in his *Aethiopis,* Lesches brings in more new heroes to fill out the ranks. He introduces Neoptolemus, the son of Achilles, and, to top that one, Eurypylus the *grandson* of Hercules! We have about thirty-three lines from this epic, and I wish there were more.

After the "Little Iliad" comes the *Iliupersis* (the "Sack of Troy"), which was written in two books, of which twelve lines survive. Arctinus is also supposed to have written this one, which tells how the Trojan Horse trick worked and describes the fall of Troy, the burning of the city, and the departure of the Greeks with their captives. There are only twelve lines extant.

The *Nostoi,* or "Returns," follows. Agias, or Hagias, of Troezen is the reputed author of this epic, which helps to fill the gap of ten years between the close of the *Iliad* and the opening of the *Odyssey*. It tells what happened to various of the heroes—such as Neoptolemus, Menelaus, and Nestor—and includes the famous tale of the murder of Agamemnon by his wife's lover, Aegisthus, and the story of the revenge of Orestes. Originally done in five books, the ancient commentators on the *Nostoi* quote only four lines from it.

The *Odyssey*, of course, follows with the tale of Odysseus and his very roundabout homeward route. The plot is far too well known for me to repeat it here, but let me point out that Homer did leave a few threads of the plot dangling. He never said what happened after the slaying of the suitors and gave no hint as to the ultimate fate of Odysseus. Eugammon of Cyrene (who lived about 568 B.C.) took it upon himself to answer these questions in his *Telegonia,* a poem in two books, which tells how Odysseus got involved in a war of the Thresprotians. When the god Ares routs Odysseus' army, he returns to Ithaca, having fathered a son named Polypoetes by Callidice, queen of the

Thesprotians. Meanwhile Telegonus, a son he fathered in the *Odyssey* days upon Circe, comes searching for his long-lost father and lands on Ithaca with a force of troops. Odysseus fights and is slain by Telegonus, neither knowing who the other is, in a sort of Sohrab-and-Rustum case of mistaken identities. Grieving, Telegonus carries the body of his dead father back to Circe's magic island, bringing Penelope and Telemachus along. On the island, Telemachus marries Circe and Telegonus marries Penelope, and all live happily forever after—literally, since Circe makes them all immortal.

This tale ends the Trojan cycle, but there were a few other epics in no particular order, such as the *Phocais,* the *Expedition of Amphiaraus,* and the *Oechalias Alosis* ("the taking of Oechalia")—all three of which are attributed to Homer—and the *Margites,* of which about six lines have survived. We also have some information on a few epics which are no longer extant and were never listed among the cyclic poems, such as a poem by Eumelus of Corinth (also one of the reputed authors of the *Titanomachia* discussed above), called the *Corinthiaca.* We know little about it: it may have contained the story of Bellerophon, who tamed the winged horse Pegasus and fought the Chimera. Considering that Bellerophon's home town was Corinth—and noting the title of this poem—we can make a pretty sound guess as to the plot of this lost epic, which was obviously concerned with the mythological history of Corinth. There is also an epic called the *Heracleia,* composed in the sixth century B.C. by Panyassis, the uncle of the historian Herodotus. The day of the Greek epic was just about over.

Greece declined as other and newer nations rose to power, such as the Macedonian empire of Philip and Alexander, which became a world-dominating power in a single lifetime and began to decline almost immediately.

As soon as Alexander, its godlike founder, died of pneumonia in Babylon in 323 B.C. at the age of only thirty-three, the empire, which sprawled across considerable portions of three continents, passed into the hands of his chief lieutenants, who became so enmeshed in trying to grab the whole realm away from each other that they did not notice its disintegration. As soon as they became aware of the situation, the Successors (as they were called) each became so involved in trying to grab one of the pieces for himself that they had no time to spare toward trying to put it back together again.

But before the Greek epic was over, it had established a powerful literary tradition. Some of the elements visible in J. R. R. Tolkien's work can be seen as far back as these cyclic poems: the world conception, a sprawling landscape with fantastic wars and imaginary places, inhabited by ferocious and fantastic monsters and curious peoples, dominated by divinities of superhuman powers. The concept of the story laid amid purely invented surroundings had been born.

Most of the rest of classical literature pursues very different concepts. Personal love lyrics, works of serious history, art criticism, letters, dramas based on the semiimaginary history of a nation or a city—all that was involved. Only in the epic was imagination permitted to run free. And in those long poems about the heroic adventures of stalwart warriors amid weird cities and bewildering monsters the notion of fantasy was born.

11.

Fantasy in the
Chanson de Geste

Says Oliver: "Pagans in force abound,
While of us Franks but very few I count;
Comrade Rollant, your horn I pray you sound!
If Charles hear, he'll turn his armies round."
Answers Rollant: "A fool I should be found;
In France the Douce would perish my renown.
With Durendal I'll lay on thick and stout,
In blood the blade, to its golden hilt, I'll drown.
Felon pagans to th' pass shall not come down;
I pledge you now, to death they all are bound."
The Song of Roland (C. S. Moncrieff translation)

Ptolemy got Egypt and Seleucus got Babylonia when
the Empire collapsed, and some of the others got it
in the neck; and the poets were too busy trying to
keep out of the way of this or that invading army to
have the leisure to write much.

But Ptolemy, and those who came after him to the
throne of Egypt, had an ear for good epic verse. An
early Ptolemy established the great Library at Alexan-
dria, the newly built capital of Egypt, and began collecting all of the cyclic epics. Here they came to be arranged in chronological order by Zenodotus, chief li-
brarian at this greatest and earliest book repository of
the ancient world (the library of Assur-bani-pal, which
was small by comparison).

Apollonius Rhodius ("of Rhodes"), who became
head of the Library after Zenodotus, was involved in a
scholarly feud with the poet Callimachus. This was in

the third century B.C., long after Arctinus and Lesches and the other Cyclic poets. Callimachus held the opinion that the epic spirit had left the Greeks. In fact, he went so far as to assert that it was no longer possible to write poems as long as the old epics. Perhaps he felt the future of heroic narrative verse to lie in the direction of the *epyllia,* or miniature epics only a few hundred lines long, such as the *Shield of Hercules* by Hesiod. Apollonius disagreed; he saw no reason why epics could no longer be written and he said as much. To prove his point, Apollonius wrote an epic of his own, the story of Jason and the Argonauts and their quest for the Golden Fleece. The *Argonautica* is the first Greek epic written after Homer which still survives. Unfortunately those who felt with Callimachus on this point could argue that, while it might technically still be possible to write at epic length, it was more than likely that the result would be inadequate; for the sad fact is that the *Argonautica* is filled with elaborate mythological allusions and pedantic notes; it is rather brief as epics go; complete in four books, it runs to about 7,000 lines, whereas the *Iliad* has over 15,000 verses. While the Jason story is certainly ripe material for an epic, this one was a failure. Even the characters are dull; the only one with any life is Medea. Longinus and Quintilian called it mediocre.

However, Varro of Atax, a contemporary of Catullus, paid it the supreme compliment of imitation when he wrote his own long Argonaut epic. So did no less a poet than Virgil himself (in Book IV of the *Aeneid*), and also Valerius Flaccus, who wrote the earliest surviving Argonaut epic in Latin. Valerius, who wrote about 93 A.D., was a Roman priest belonging to the college that had charge of the famous Sibylline Books that were supposed to prophesy the future of Rome. And, very much later, about 1572 A.D., Ronsard was to imitate Apollonius of Rhodes in his attempt at composing a French "antional epic," the *Françiade*.

Now that the Rhodian poet had proved it could be done, a few other Greeks tried their hand at the same game. One of the last to make a real stab at it—far too late to prevent the decline and death of Greek as the grand epic language—was Quintus Smyrnaeus, who went straight back to the old cyclic poets for his scenery.

Quintus of Smyrna, in his *Posthomerica* (or what happened "after Homer"—i.e. after the *Iliad*), covered very much the same general ground as several of the above-mentioned cyclic epics, such us the *Aethiopis* of Arctinus of Miletus, the *Iliasmikra* or Little Iliad of Lesches of Mitylene, and the *Iliupersis,* also ascribed to Arctinus. In fact, it is considered quite likely that Quintus had the texts of the lost epic poems in front of him as he worked, for they were still extant in his day.

Quintus proved not only that Apollonius was right —that epics could still be written in the old-fashioned way—but also that the critics of the *Argonautica* were wrong in predicting failure for subsequent efforts. In short, Quintus' epic is not only pretty good poetry, filled with color and excitement and striking imagery, told with scope and sweep, and a nice eye for detail, but it tells a gripping story, to boot.* It teems with the

---

* A sample, will indicate something of the flavor. This is from Book VII, lines 297–311, of the Arthur S. Way translation.

> Beware, my child,
> Peril of waters when thou sailest back
> From Troy or other shores, such as beset
> Full oftentimes the voyagers that ride

stuff of heroics—gore-drenched battlefields, thrilling duels between the heroes, storms at sea, supernatural apparitions from the grave, eerie prophecies, and the like.

Nevertheless, the day of the Greek epic was just about over. The epic impulse traveled to Rome by way of Livius Andronicus, who translated the *Odyssey* into Latin meters in the last half of the third century B.C.—an event which is considered the beginning of the epic in the Roman world. Naevius, a little later, composed an epic on the First Punic War. Then came Ennius, about a century later.

Latin poetry really begins with Ennius, about 240 B.C. His *Annals* traced the history of Rome from the beginning to his own lifetime. The epic verse is rather primitive, but it nobly explored the potentials of Latin as a sonorous poetic medium, and those who came after him owe much to his pioneer work.

Callimachus, who had argued that long epics were impossible, and those who felt, as he did, that the future lay with the *epyllia,* had a brief day. Everybody tried their hand at the *epyllion;* Cato the Censor wrote a *Lydia* and a *Diana,* Calvus an *Io,* Catullus a *Marriage of Peleus and Thetis,* Cinna a *Zmyrna,* and so on, drawing their plots from ancient mythology. But

---

The long sea-ridges, when the sun hath left
The Archer-star, and meets the misty Goat.
When the wild blasts drive on the lowering storm,
Or when Orion to the darkling west
Slopes into Ocean's river sinking slow.
Beware the time of equal days and nights,
When blasts that o'er the sea's abysses rush—
None knoweth whence—in fury of battle clash.
Beware the Pleiads' setting, when the sea
Maddens beneath their power—nor these alone,
But other stars, terrors of hapless men,
As o'er the wide sea-gulf they set or rise.

roughly contemporaneous with Catullus (who lived
from 87 to 54 B.C.) was the epic poet Lucretius (99 to
55 B.C.), author of a didactic epic called the *De
Rerum Natura*. Then came the great Virgil (70 to 19
B.C.), who tried to equal the Homeric sublimity and
came very close. He, like Homer, opens his epic *in
media res*, "in the middle of the story"; a subsequent
flashback recapitulates the beginning. He also imitates
the great *nekyuia*, or calling-up-a-ghost scene, like the
one in Book XI of the *Odyssey* where Odysseus summons up the spirit of the old seer Teiresias. He includes other Homeric touches, such as the Catalogue
of Ships and the Council of the Gods. And, following
the example of the cyclic poets, he grafted his *Aeneid*
onto the Troy Tale, taking for the hero of his epic a
minor character, Aineias, mentioned briefly in the second book of Homer's *Iliad*.

Next came Manilius (about 20 B.C. to 25 A.D.) and
Lucan (39 to 65 A.D.). Lucan's epic was historical, although florid and gory, a work about the civil wars of
Caesar and Pompey, known to us as the *Pharsalia*,
after the plains of Pharsalus, where the Civil War was
decided (the real title is *De Bello Civili*, "On the Civil
Wars"). Then came Statius (40 to 95 A.D.), who
wrote a *Thebaid* which closely imitates Virgil and
began an *Achilleis* but only lived to complete one and
a half books of it.*

While the Roman epic poets imitated either Homer
or Virgil or both, they were not, on the whole, very
successful. Most of these poems simply cannot stand
comparison with the Greeks, who had a light and airy

---

* Many other writers tried an Achilles epic. Goethe wrote one in
1797.

imagination much given to "winged flights," while the
Romans were heavy-handed, pragmatic, and, for the
most part, just plain dull. And there is nothing duller
than a dull Latin epic! *

As the Roman Empire began to fade, the epic—the
formal, classical epic as a serious artform—declined
and was lost until it was revived in post-Carolingian
Europe.

The greater part of epic literature was completely
lost as civilizations collapsed and empires decayed.
Some were irretrievably destroyed, like the cyclic epics.
Others were mislaid for a time, like the *Posthomerica*
of Quintus of Smyrna, a manuscript copy of which
finally turned up in the fifteenth century, when Cardi-
nal Bessario discovered it moldering in a convent library at Otranto in Calabria.

When the concept of epic poetry, together with
some good specimens, traveled into Europe, this cul-
tural cross-fertilization stimulated a harvest of interesting works. But after Statius, the heroic epic declined
until revived by Petrarch in 1341 with his *Africa*. But
the younger nations of post-Roman Europe had an ancient traditional heroic literature all their own, and as
they rose to power these old heroic lays began to be

---

* An example is the *Punica* of Silius Italicus (26–101 A.D.), a ponderous and unreadable historical epic laid during the Second Punic
War. Silius worshiped the memory of Virgil (so much so that he
personally bought the site of Virgil's grave in Naples and restored
it). He steeped himself in Virgiliana, but little seems to have soaked
in. The *Punica* is one of the dullest works ever written—as the Ger-
mans say about the *Hortulus Animae;* "es lässt sich nicht lesen,"
which literally means, "it does not permit itself to be read." This
judgment holds despite the work's exciting subject and exotic lo-
cales, such as the luxurious African metropolis of Carthage, which
Flaubert put to splendid use in his lush romance *Salammbô*. The
Punica does have one claim to fame: with 12,000 verses, it is the
longest single epic in Latin literature.

written down, resulting in whole new epic literatures which owed only a little to the classical epics.

These indigenous writings included the Anglo-Saxon *Beowulf,* written down in the dialect spoken in eleventh-century Wessex from an original probably composed in Northumbria toward the end of the seventh century A.D. *Beowulf* is a brilliant poem—it is considered the first great work in British literature—and a splendid adventure story, filled with hideous trolls, enchanted swords, magic armor, fire-breathing dragons, and the like, oddly enough based on actual history. Beowulf himself is now considered a historical personage, although we know little about him other than the fact that he fought with his chief, Hygelac, in an actual raid against the Franks and Frisians about 520 A.D.

France produced the *Chanson de Roland,* an anonymous eleventh-century French epic of some 4,000 lines which has been called the first good poem of any scope in French literature. Like Beowulf, Roland is a historical figure—we know of a Count Hrodlandt of the Breton Marches, who fell at the historical battle of Roncesvalles, fought on August 15, 778 A.D. Both Beowulf and Roland have cognominal swords—famous magic weapons with names and histories attached to them (Beowulf's Hrunting and Roland's Durendal, which once belonged to Hector of Troy).

The *Song of Roland* and a vast number of subsequent French epics are called *chansons de geste* ("songs of deeds"). They form the central body of what can be referred to as the Carolingian Mythos. Gautier compiled a list of 110 in all.

Roland, according to the mythos, was one of the Twelve Peers or Twelve Paladins who served Charlemagne—a group of knightly heroes of great renown gathered about their King, much as the Knights of the Round Table were allied to King Arthur. Authorities are not in agreement as to the names of these Twelve Peers. The *Song of Roland* itself lists them (*laisse* LXIV): Count Roland, nephew of King Charlemagne; his good friend and companion Oliver; Archbishop Turpin of Rheims; Gerin; Count Geriers; Gerart of Roussillon; Engeliers of Gascony; Duke Samson; Anselm the Proud; Otes; Count Gaultiers; Berengiers.*

Since the *Song of Roland* kills off most of these people, it would seem that the French epic would have to end right at the start. Not so. For, once *Roland* was hitting the medieval equivalent of the best-seller lists, the trouvères (bards) began composing epics laid in a period earlier than the Roland—"prequels," like those Greek epics we were discussing earlier. Many dealt with the heroes in their youth, among them *Enfances Roland* and *Enfances Ogier*. There are also epics about each of the Peers—verse biographies, so to speak, like *Chevalerie Ogier de Danemarche* (composed between 1192 and 1200 A.D.), *Girart de Roussillon* (circa 1160–1170), and *Garin de Monglane* (second half of the thirteenth century). Some epics dealt with Charlemagne, and some with his son (such as *Couronnement de Louis*, after 1130).

Soon whole schools of poets began to create entire cycles of *chansons*. There was a "William of Orange"

---

* However, elsewhere in the same poem are mentioned such Peers as Geoffrey of Anjou, Duke Naimes, Tybalt of Rheims, Ogier the Dane, Count Acolin of Gascony, Richard the Old and his nephew Henry, Milun, Ivon, Ivor, Otto, and an otherwise unidentified Duke of burgundy—another twelve. The various *chansons* written as sequels to *Roland* include such additional Peers as Huon of Bordeaux, Thierry of Anjou, Berat de Mondidier, Aubri the Burgundian, and William the Scot.

cycle, with about eight epics in all; a "Garin de Monglane" cycle, made up of some sixteen epics; a cycle
about "Aymeri de Narbonne" (father of William of
Orange), consisting of at least eight more epics; and so
on. Although there are more than 100 French epics
which grew up around this Carolingian legend, except
for the *Roland,* which is a genuine masterpiece, and
one or two others,* they have not been translated into
English.

Charlemagne—Karl, King of the Franks, called
Carolus Magnus (Charles the Great; i.e. Charlemagne)—really lived, of course. He was a historical
monarch, born in 742 and dying in 814 A.D., son of
Pepin the Short, who took over from Childerich III at
the end of the Merovingian dynasty. Charlemagne was
one of the great rulers, founder of the short-lived but
splendid Carolingian Empire, ruler of all of France,
most of what we would today call Germany, and about
half of Italy, to say nothing of a considerable part of

---

* Such as the first in the "William" cycle, *Chanson de Guillaume,*
which was composed perhaps as early as 1070–1080 A.D., or a trifle
later. An English verse translation, *The Song of William,* by Edward Noble Stone, was published in 1951. It is a spirited poem, not
without color and a certain quality of gusto. The following sample
may convey the style. The scene occurs in *laisse* CXLV, where Ted-
bald is arming and riding out to do battle with the wicked Paynim
King:

> Then a hauberk fair on his body they placed,
> And a helmet green to his head they laced,
>   His sword he girded, the bright blade hung;
> His mighty shield by the band he clasped,
> His lance so keen in his right hand grasped,
>   White, to the ground, the banneret swung.
> Then a steed of Castile before him they led,
>   On the left by the stirrup he mounted straightway;
> Forth by the postern gate hath he sped,
> Ten thousand behind, helm on head,
>   In Archamp seeking King Deramé.

the Slavic and Balkan area. His empire did not last very long after he died, but it was remembered—in fact, it became a legend, looked back on as a golden age of stability and power. Naturally legends began to attach themselves to Charlemagne's memory.* And out of this, in a century or two, grew a whole epic literature.

Much the same literary process was, of course, taking place elsewhere at about the same time. National literatures were being founded around central works, such as the Spanish national epic, *Poema de mio Cid,* a work of unknown authorship which dates from the mid-1100's. This heroic epic (*cantar de gesta,* as the Spaniards called the genre) is based not on legend but on more recent history, as was the Roman Lucan's *Pharsalia.* The epic celebrates the deeds of "El Cid Campeador"—the historical warrior Ruy Diaz de Bivar (1040?–1099), who fell fighting the Moors like the Frankish knight, Roland.

The Portuguese also drew the theme for their national epic from history. This work, *The Lusiads,*† is a heroic narrative about the history of the Portuguese people, interwoven with tales of the epic voyages of discovery of Vasco da Gama. The author is Luís de Camoens (1524?–1580).

While *The Lusiads* is a Virgilian epic, the day of the

---

* Between wars, conquests, and the like, he found time to marry five wives (Hildegard, Luitgard, Desiderata, Fastrada, and Himiltrud; there was also a mistress named Adelinda). With such a marital record, it's no surprise that he fathered five sons and four daughters.

† The title refers to the Portuguese people themselves. In the original it is *Os Lusíadas,* the "Sons of Lusus," i.e. the Lusitanians or Portuguese.

classical epic was at its end. Native epics were rising, drawn from native history of folklore and written in the native languages. These poems, with the French *chansons,* represent not so much a revival of classical form as a debasement and corruption of the epic which had descended to a lower level of artistic effort. From the highwater mark of the *Song of Roland* the French poems decayed into jingly verse chronicles. At length these latter-day quasi-epics proved so unsatisfactory as to stimulate into growth the development of a wholly new form of epic-derived literature which demanded a lesser degree of poetic genius on the part of the author and a minuscule knowledge of classical mythology or history on the part of the reader, together with a less intense and sophisticated degree of artistic interest.

In other words, the formal epic had decayed into the *chanson,* which soon descended to the romance.

What had the Renaissance poets added to the growth of the epic fantasy? They picked up from the classical poets the notions of heroic characters wandering and warring through a world peopled by strange animals, curious people, and fantastic monsters. But to this they added several elements which also turn up in Tolkien: cognominal weapons—that is, famous swords with names and histories, like Roland's Durendal and Charlemagne's Joyeuse and the Cid's Colada and Tizona. The supernatural element was now supplied, not so much by the pagan gods, but by elves, fairies, dwarves, and ghostly apparitions. Magical talismans, enchanted swords and armor and the like became popular.

These elements were not to coalesce in the materials

of pure fantasy, however, either in classical epic or Renaissance *chanson,* but in the great romances of the late Middle Ages, which we shall examine in the next chapter.

12.

Fantasy in the
Medieval Romance

> Many romances men make new
> Of valiant knights, both strong and true;
> Of Roland and of Oliver,
> And all the other famous peers;
> Of Alexander and Charlemagne;
> And of King Arthur and Gawain,
> How courtesy these knights sustained,
> Of Turpin and Oger the Dane.
> *The Romance of Richard the Lion-Hearted*
> (Bradford B. Broughton translation)

~~~~~~~~~~~~~~~~~

We call them "Romances" because they were written in what are known as the Romance languages, i.e. such tongues as Spanish, or Italian, or French, which grew out of Latin, the "Roman" language.

Romances were very widely popular throughout the Middle Ages and were so numerous that the result is a heroic literature much larger both in size and in influence than the Graeco-Roman epic literature—although smaller, of course, in content of artistic genius.*

As mentioned above, the *chanson de geste* borrowed certain successful devices from heroic narrative and passed these along to the romance. Among these are

---

* I imagine people started writing prose epics (romances) because it was easier to control than formal epic meter, which is pretty exhausting stuff and takes remarkable talent to do successfully. As Alexander Pope put it: "verse loitered into prose."

the larger-than-life hero, heroine, and villain, as well as the strong element of the supernatural, the occasional act of direct divine intervention into mortal affairs, and the preoccupation with the dual epic themes of quest and warfare as standard plot motifs.

But the romance also incorporated a heterogeneous mass of story material that was not only unknown to the formal epic but was even alien and inimical to it. One of these new features is the archetype of the wizard or the magician. Magicians are almost completely unknown in the breadth of epic literature and did not enter the field in any numerical strength until the evolution of the romance, which popularized them. This is not to say that wizards (of a sort) did not exist in classical times, for they did, in the form of alchemists and diviners, astrologers, dream readers, and the like. But they played no part in the cast of the typical epic.

Another new element is the use of magic per se. There is hardly any magic in the Greek or Roman epic. There the supernatural element consists very largely of such fantastic monsters and hybrids as the Chimera, the Hydra, and Charybdis and Scylla, as well as the occasional conjuring up of the spirits of the dead (or, conversely, the descent of this or that hero into the Netherworld, like Hercules and Orpheus) and the appearances and actions of the gods and Immortals. Magic—that is, the powers of witch and wizard, the employment of charmed weapons, spells and talismans and the like—was foreign to the spirit of the classical epics (which to a considerable extent were considered religious works; Homer, indeed, was most certainly regarded by the Greeks as the "Old Testament" of their religion; Hesiod, in the *Theogony,* though not the *Works and Days,* served as a sort of "New Testament," * and Virgil was eventually considered what we of today would call an "inspired, prophetic writer").

You can see that what I have called the "debasement" of the epic into the romance was even reflected in the details of the plot elements. Magic is, after all, a debasement of religion, in which the charm is substituted for the prayer. (And if any reader wants to challenge the above flat statement that the wizard was alien to epic literature by pointing to the witch Circe in the *Odyssey,* or Odysseus' conversation with the shade of the wizard Teiresias during the "descent into Hades" scene in the same epic, remember that Circe, sorceress or no, was a goddess, daughter of Helios the Sun God, and that the blind seer Teiresias was a prophet of Apollo.)

Although the romances toyed occasionally with the Matter of Troy, their plots were usually taken from such European folklore as the Arthurian cycle or the legends of Charlemagne and the Twelve Peers or from the fabulous history of Alexander the Great, who became a wonder-working knightly hero to the medieval writers. The foremost place among romances is held by *Amadis of Gaul,* one of the most delightful fantasies ever written and one of the most influential books of all time—so influential, in fact, that an entire literature

---

* The religion of the ancient Greeks was remarkably civilized, sophisticated, and tolerant. It had no sacred scriptures (such as were common among Oriental religions like Judaism and Christianity), very little in the way of revealed dogma, and no hierarchial church structure to speak of. The Olympian myth served mostly as a source for poets and dramatists and was useful in lending a trifle of supernatural authority to support the state and its institutions. No one was ever burned for heresy among the Greeks, unlike the "civilized" inhabitants of Christian Europe. Socrates, who was martyred by his countrymen, was condemned for corruptive moral influences on the young rather than for his lack of religious orthodoxy.

sprang from it, and its influence can be seen at work to this day.

The date and authorship of *Amadis,* and the matter of its original language—Spanish or Portuguese—is still under dispute. Tradition ascribes it to a Portuguese named Vasco de Lobeira, of the era of Ferdinand of Portugal who died in 1385. Modern scholarship inclines, however, towards a Galician knight, Joao de Lobeira, who frequented the court of Portugal between 1258 and 1285. However, there is *no* question about the amazing power and fertility of this astonishing work as it survived in a prose version at around 1500. Ariosto and Montaigne admired it, and Cervantes praised it as "best of all the books of this kind that have ever been written," while the Italian epic poet Torquato Tasso called it "the most beautiful and perhaps the most profitable story of its kind that can be read."

The world of *Amadis* is simply splendid: a crowded and gorgeous tapestry filled with marvelous and intricate detailwork. Strange palaces of moon-pale marble, white as carven ice, rise on the shadowy edges of enchanted forests drowned in mystic purple gloom, wherein dwell rough and desperate bandits or malignant sorcerers. Velvet meadows are brilliant with silken pavilions, the air bright with the gilded blazonry of banners, where steel armor glitters amid gem-studded gold crowns. Profound and perilous gorges lie beneath castle-crested hills, and far beyond soar the blue and jagged peaks of dragon-haunted mountains. Hideous giants dwell in the far-off peaks or on the shadowy and uncharted islands which rise from pale, mist-wreathed seas. The tale of *Amadis* is one of enormous variety, told with verve and skill, with an eye for color and detail. The knight Amadis, son of King Perion of Gaul and of Elisena, daughter to Garinter of Brittany, is raised by a lonely Scots knight in ignorance of his kingly heritage. He becomes one of the boldest heroes at the court of King Lisuarte of Britain and falls in love with Oriana the Fair. Strange forces move about him: he is the focus of the Powers of Good and of Evil —represented by a mysterious, veiled sorceress of vast thaumaturgical skills, Urganda the Unknown, and a cunning and truly magnificent villain, the magician Archelaus.

The four books of *Amadis of Gaul* are filled with knightly quests, dangerous voyages, ferocious battles and invasions, intrigue and treachery. At length Amadis and Oriana wed, he is restored to his long-lost parents, and the story comes to a dramatic conclusion with the destruction of Archelaus.

The story was so ingenious, so filled with peril and magic and mystery, and either so unlike anything that had been written before it or so clearly superior to its predecessors that it became enormously famous. Montalvo, whose published Spanish version of 1508 survives, enthusiastically wrote a fifth book and tacked it on to his retelling of the original four. This fifth book, "Esplandian," deals with the adventures of the heroic son of Amadis. It introduces new characters who are little more than variants on the original cast: for example, replacing Archelaus the Enchanter is his mother, Arcobane, "a witch deeply versed in the mysteries of the occult arts." Still further on, Montalvo drags in Archelaus' older brother, Matroed.

Esplandian falls in love with Leonorina, Princess of Byzantium, but powerful enemies are at work—such as a beautiful but impetuous Queen of the Amazons, who wages war against the Princess, bringing to the fray a squadron of fifty well-trained griffins which fly over the city like a flight of dive bombers, belching fire and smoke upon the heads of the unhappy citizens below.

Hardly had Montalvo finished "Esplandian" and published it as part of *Amadis,* than still more spurious additions were attached to the ever-growing novel. There was a sixth book, concerned with the adventures of Florisando, the nephew of Amadis. Then, in 1526, came the seventh and eighth books, whose author is believed to be one Juan Diaz. These two are about Lisuarte of Greece (son of Esplandian and grandson of Amadis), and his partner, Perion, whom Diaz sets forth as a later-born second son of Amadis and Oriana. The ninth book, "Amadis of Greece," was published only nine years later and tells of the grandson of the original Amadis and of his love for Niquea, the Queen of Babylon. Their son, Florisel, is the protagonist of the tenth book, which introduces more of the family, like Florisel's Amazonian sister, a powerful woman of quarrelsome nature and a mean left, named Alastraxare; plus his Aunt Sylvia, who has a torrid romance with Prince Anastarax, whom the potent witch Zirfea had locked up for life in a fiery palace. In the end, everybody gets married and Florisel begets a daughter named Diana who is the heroine of the eleventh and twelfth books of this interminable super-super-novel—Diana being the great-great-great-granddaughter of the original Amadis.

In the eleventh volume, "Agesilan of Colchos," the hero sets out on a world-spanning search for his lost love, Diana. In the course of his travels he saves the poor old blind king of the Garamantes, who is starving to death because, without his sight, he cannot avoid a wicked dragon who is stealing his food right out from under his nose. The entire episode is a straight theft from a scene in *Orlando Furioso* (canto xxxiii, stanza 102 ff) in which Senapus, King of Ethiopia, suffers from a like misfortune and has his daily rations intercepted by a band of harpies until Astolpho comes along to help.*

The twelfth and last volume of this series is about Silvio de la Selva, the son of Amadis of Greece and a certain Finistea. But the story goes on through the adventures of Rogel of Greece, his son Spheramond; and then there's Amadis of Astre, the son of Agesilan, and so on.

Having grown from a single volume to half a library shelf, *Amadis of Gaul* must be at least three times as long as the complete Tolkien trilogy and ten times as complicated. But even this is not the end of it, for, beside the out-and-out "continuations" of the original story described above, there were an enormous number of just plain imitations. Romance after romance poured off the presses of Europe: *Palmerin of England, Tirante the White, Platir, Primaleon, Parthenopex of the Wood, Olivante de Laura, Belianus of Greece, Felixmarte of Hyrcania,* and others beyond my patience to list.

Each new author tried to outdo the other by piling

---

* In point of fact, Ariosto himself took the whole idea from the story of Phineus and the harpies in Apollonius Rhodius' *Argonautica*. A good idea is a good idea, after all—and in those days it was perfectly acceptable, indeed it was almost part of one tradition, to re-tell, to use again, to repeat: it was in the telling, as in the aural tradition, that one's artistry and individuality became apparent.

marvel upon marvel, superlative upon superlative, by presenting a more crowded, and bewildering plot than those of the romances of the previous year. Finally they were all borrowing from each other, until things got to the point where the entire literary movement was hopelessly confused.

Most of these sequels and imitations are of Spanish, Portuguese, or Catalonian origin. They are not very good, although they were highly popular with the people of their time. *Amadis* towered above them all in power of narrative and imaginative fertility. So severe a critic of the romance as Miguel de Cervantes (who was to ruthlessly lampoon the whole ridiculous school in *Don Quixote*) even singled out *Amadis* for praise. In Part I, Chapter VI, the local curate and the barber are going through Don Quixote's library to purge it of unwholesome books. Of all the tomes collected by the ingenious gentleman of la Mancha, they spare only three from the flames: *Tirante the White* for its "quaintness," *Palmerin of England* for its merits and because Cervantes mistakenly fancied its author to have been a King of Portugal, and first and foremost of all, *Amadis*. Speaking through the mouth of the barber, Cervantes hailed *Amadis* in these words: "This is the best of all the books of this kind that have ever been written."

One of the things wrong with the imitators of Lobeira's masterpiece is that they could not risk killing off Amadis himself, so popular a character had he become to the readers of his time. Instead of decently permitting the aged hero to go to his reward, they kept him alive, although they usually relegated him to the background. He goes on and on for attenuated generations, rather like Zal and Rustum in the Persian national epic, the *Shah Namah.* In that book, long after Rustum, the son of Zal, has grown to manhood and fathered Sohrab, who in turn fathers a son who grew up and marries and becomes himself a father, the poet Firdausi keeps the superannuated founder of the clan, Zal, lingering on and on for about two hundred years. There is something touching in this—an author not having the heart to kill off a fine old hero—but it does not make for good writing.*

The enormous popular success of the Iberian school of chivalric romance almost met its match in Italy, where a comparable group of heroic poets arose about the same time or a little after.

The most important of the early Italian romancers was Luigi Pulci (1432–1484), author of a burlesque heroic poem called *Morgante Maggiore,* which, although popular with contemporary readers, left little mark on fantastic literature. It mainly served to pave the way for a greater and more serious writer of romance, named Count Matteo Maria Boiardo (?1434–1494). Boiardo (or Bojardo), drawing from Carolingian sources, composed for the amusement of his patron, Duke Ercole d'Este and the ducal court, an extravagant romance called *Orlando Innamorato* (Roland in Love), whose plot he derived from the *Fabulous Chronicle* of Bishop Turpin, or "pseudo-Turpin," as the historians of literature call him. This romance was left unfinished by Boiardo's death, but the story

---

* It is generally conceded that the sequels to *Amadis* are vastly inferior. The English poet Robert Southey, who did a standard English prose translation of *Amadis,* wisely refrained from translating any of the sequels so clumsily grafted onto the original books. He comments, rather succinctly, that Boiardo's *Orlando Innamorato* (discussed below) was the only story in literature to have ever been successfully continued by other hands.

was picked up by Ludovico Ariosto (1474–1533) when he wrote his great romantic poem, *Orlando Furioso.* As with the original four books of *Amadis,* we are dealing with a genuine masterpiece in discussing the great *Orlando Furioso,* and although the poem has been translated into English more than once, only summarized editions are presently available.

Ariosto's version of the golden age of Charlemagne is a far cry from that given in the *Song of Roland.* Among the Twelve Peers strange new faces shine, new characters complicate the plot. Angelica, daughter of the Emperor of Cathay, wins the love of Orlando but spurns him, driving him to madness. Astolpho flies to the moon on a griffin borrowed from the magician Atalante, in order to bring back Orlando's lost wits. Bradamante the Lady Knight and Malagigi the Dwarf-Enchanter, Mandrocardo the Tartar, and a host of others fill the story with fresh excitement and some spectacular scenes, such as the visit of Astolpho to the kingdom of Prester John in Africa, where he sees the Source of the Nile and watches herds of tame unicorns grazing on the palace lawn. Spenser, Voltaire, and Goethe were fascinated by Ariosto's fertile imagination and sense of color and drama.

The whole romance genre became corrupt very swiftly, partly owing to the need of every romancer to outdo his brethren in the craft with more violent excesses, and partly because of radical transplantation of a corpus of national folklore from one culture to another, where it was crudely and forcibly grafted onto the native product.

For example, this attenuation happened when the Italian school began writing pseudo-Arthurian romances. The Arthurian romance itself is a conglomerate, a bastard outgrowth of various elements from Celtic, Welsh, British, and French folklore. When the florid Italians began meshing this material with other traditions, mixing Merlin and Charlemagne and Amadis in the same tale, and injecting transfusions of really alien plot elements* some amazing oddities resulted. An example of the appalling kind of literary smorgasbord that resulted is a strange opus, *The Perceforest,* a vast, unwieldy prose compilation that ties up the Grail quests and Prester John with the legendary exploits of Alexander the Great. Happily, I think, *The Perceforest* has never been rendered into modern English.

Even Ariosto's mighty poem itself, work of imaginative genius or no, is still a peculiar mixture. Its title echoes the "wrath of Achilles" in Homer; its characters are drawn from Charlemagne's France in part, partly from Arthur's Britain, and partly from native Italian folklore; and they all go chasing each other madly across the world from Tartary to Africa, from Cathay to the moon†—and back—like a foreshadowing of *Baron Munchausen.* This powerful but pixilated poem was translated into English verse by Sir John Harington (1560–1612), a courtier and godson of Queen Elizabeth. The translation was published only 58 years after Ariosto's death, a good indication of the work's popularity. The qualities of Harington's verse

---

* Such as genies and peris from the *Arabian Nights* and echoes of distant bodies of legend. Orlando's sword once belonged to Hector of Troy; Boiardo attributes to one of his characters, Gradosso, armor which had belonged to the Biblical hero Samson; and so on.

† Pictured as a sort of "land of the lost," where everything that earth mislays is kept. Thither flies the knight Astolpho on a hippogriff, which had belonged to the magician Atalantes, in search of Roland's wits. He cleverly and rightly assumed that, since the hero had temporarily "lost his reason," it could be located on the moon.

have, on occasion, been called into question, as by Ben Jonson, who told a friend: "John Harington's Ariosto under all translations was the worst."

By this time the whole literature of romance was so hopelessly mixed up (not to say bogged down) that the death blow came from Edmund Spenser not long after. Ariosto used the traditional eight-line stanza popular with Italian verse, the *ottava rima,* which was admirably suited to the needs of a rapidly moving story, aided in swift transitions of scene, and gave a natural limit to the episodes. These qualities, plus Ariosto's ironic and sophisticated treatment of love, his unusual wit and lively story-telling abilities, made for a far more accessible work than Spenser's complex imitation which followed. Spenser, who lived about 1522–1599, borrowed almost the whole style, form, and substance of Ariosto's Italian extravaganza and transplanted the whole back into Arthur's Britain, Italian characters and all. By this time the whole tradition had lost its vitality. It hardly needed the final *coup de grace* from Cervantes' magnificent lampoon, which came shortly after. *

Tasso and Ariosto and the others, however, left a permanent mark on literature. Even neighboring arts were infected with the chivalric mythos. In painting, the seventeenth-century French artist Poussin did whole series of oils and wash drawings, such as his *Rinaldo and Armida* (1635), which are preserved in The Hermitage Museum at Leningrad, the Pushkin Museum at Moscow, the Louvre, and so on. Operatic composers such as Arconati, who wrote a flamboyant *Orlando,* found in the Italian romance a rich source

---

* The first part of *Don Quixote* was published in 1605 and the remainder in 1615.

for the kind of bravura story material best suited to their tastes. The influence has not died yet; so recent a painter as Odilon Redon (1840–1916) drew inspiration from the Italians for such works as his famous pastel *Roger and Angelica,* now in the Museum of Modern Art in New York.

13.
The Men
Who Invented Fantasy

Ah! the strange life of happiness and woe
That I have led, since my young feet did go
From that grey, peaceful, much-beloved abode,
But now, indeed, will I cast off the load
Of memory of vain hopes that came to nought,
Of rapturous joys with biting sorrows bought.
The past is past, though I cannot forget
Those days, with long life laid before me yet.
Ah, but one moment, ere I turn the page.
WILLIAM MORRIS, *The Life and Death of Jason,*
Book XVII

All the elements of heroic or epic fantasy had now been created and used: the concept of the imaginary world or land in which magic works and "gods, ghosts, and gorgons" dwell; the twin themes of the wandering adventurer or quest hero and of the war between opposed forces; even the work of fantastic literature with all the scope and grandeur of an epic. It awaited only a small number of writers to draw these elements together from epic, saga, and romance and to reintroduce them into modern fiction.

THE REFORMER

William Morris was one of those eccentric Englishmen without whom the world would be a poorer and much duller place. He was born in 1834, just three

years before Queen Victoria ascended the throne. At
once a dreamer and a doer, a sensitive British gentleman of refined artistic taste, he was also a political reformer and a hard-working, practical-minded entrepre-
neur. He lived during those difficult days when the Industrial Revolution was beginning to change man's
way of life. Everywhere he looked, Morris saw ugly
factories belching smoke, rows of dingy slums. The
green fields and quaint old towns of Britain were being
besmirched and destroyed in the name of progress.

Thoroughly disenchanted with his own era, Morris
looked backward with fond nostalgia to the Middle
Ages. He saw that world as a sort of bucolic utopia
filled with unspoiled countryside and glorious cities,
peopled by noble lords and stout foresters, great-
hearted ladies and wise kings. In other words, he saw
the Middle Ages as they had never been. In fact, the
era had been one of superstition and ignorance, pov-
erty and disease, endless petty wars and cruel persecu-
tions—an era that had little respect for human rights
or the dignity of man. But to Morris it looked like a
rose-and-golden world, and he dreamed of restoring it,
or at least of salvaging much that was good from it.

He became a pioneer socialist, a would-be political
reformer. He argued that the workingman was degraded into a slave of the factory owner; he dreamed
of reviving the tradition of hereditary crafts. Together
with such kindred artistic spirits as Dante Gabriel Ros-
setti and Morris' old school friend Sir Edward Burne-
Jones, the celebrated pre-Raphaelite painter, Morris
dabbled at everything from architecture, wood carving,
and metalwork to designing stained-glass windows,
tapestries, furniture, and wallpaper. He even illustrated, designed, and printed his own books.

But Morris' eccentricity bordered on genius, and he frequently excelled at whatever he turned his hand to. As a printer, for example, he produced the Kelmscott Chaucer, considered one of the most magnificent examples of the bookwright's art created in the nineteenth century. As a poet, at the age of twenty-four, he wrote *The Defence of Guenevere,* now recognized as one of the jewels of Victorian poetry. As a translator, he introduced whole generations of his countrymen to the splendors of the Icelandic sagas through famous translations of *The Volsunga Saga,* the *Gunnlaug Saga, Grettir's Saga,* and his own original epic poem, *Sigurd the Volsung.**

Poetry aside, Morris was also a novelist, and it is with this vocation that he becomes pertinent to this study. For in hearkening back to a glorified vision of the Middle Ages, Morris discovered the old romances and Grail quests and drew upon them for the style and substance of his own novels, which were laid in medieval times. There was nothing particularly novel in this device. Sir Walter Scott, who died two years before William Morris was born, had helped make the historical romance enduringly popular with novels like *Ivanhoe, Kenilworth,* and *The Talisman.* These books were set in the Middle Ages, in Elizabethan England, or in the era of the Crusades. But where Morris differed from Scott was in giving to his medieval romances not settings of historical eras, but imaginary

---

* George Bernard Shaw described it as the greatest epic since Homer. Actually, it is a good poem, which holds up even today, though not as great as Shaw thought it was. Morris also wrote a long verse romance called *The Life and Death of Jason* (1867), the first major treatment of the story of the quest for the Golden Fleece since Apollonius Rhodius' *Argonautica.* He translated the *Odyssey* into English verse as well.

settings. The novels of William Morris were laid in worlds of his own invention, just as the romances of Amadis and Tirante and Palmerin often stray into realms that cannot be found on any map. This was a decisive innovation. For while his fiction combined much of the antiquarian romanticism of Scott and even a touch of the eerie horror of Horace Walpole and the Gothic novelists, Morris was writing something that was basically different from either the historical novel or the novel of supernatural terrors—he had invented *the heroic fantasy novel.*

His prose style was essentially different from other novelists as well. It was simple and lucid, with an element of freshness and beauty—a springtime flavor of the high, heroic days of chivalry and splendor modeled directly on the romances and Grail quests. There is in Morris' work the same air of dim enchantment and strange mystery that can be found in the pages of Sir Thomas Malory. He was not in the tradition of English prose fiction at all, but founded a tradition of his own. His novels are set in strange, uncanny, adventurous worldscapes of magic and heroism, sometimes idyllic, sometimes touched with shadowy horror, but always new and original beyond knowledge, worlds out of space and time, in hazy romantic landscapes not to be found on any map, in eras which no history lists.

Morris' imitation of medieval prose was not overdone: clarity and simplicity and a certain haunting and lyrical music makes it very readable, as in this sample from the first chapter of *The Well at the World's End:*

Now it came to this at last, that to these young men the kingdom of their father seemed strait; and they longed to see the ways of other men, to strive for life. For though they were king's sons, they had but little world's wealth;

save and except good meat and drink, and enough or too much thereof; house-room of the best; friends to be merry with, and maidens to kiss, and these also as good as might be; freedom withal to come and go as they would; the heavens above them, the earth to bear them up, and the meadows and acres, the woods and fair streams and the little hills of Upmeads, for that was the name of their country and kingdom.

What Morris had done was to go Scott and the other historical novelists one better by telling a tale of earlier days in the very style and tradition of those days. In novels like *The House of the Wulfings* (1889), *The Wood Beyond the World* (1895), *The Well at the World's End* (1896), and *The Water of the Wondrous Isles* (1897) he created immense and curious worldscapes thronged with marvelous cities and strange beasts, peopled with powerful enchantresses and valiant bandits, with young knight-errants of courage and courtesy, bound on long and perilous quests and curious adventures. For in adopting the language and tone of a more remote epoch, William Morris also adopted the supernaturalism and magic of such an epoch. And in so doing he laid the foundations of fantasy literature.

It must be kept in mind that the poets of the Homeric age believed in their gods and monsters. While the classical epics read as fantasies to the modern reader, they were not deliberately made fantastic by the men who wrote them. This is true to a lesser extent of the authors of the *chansons de geste* or the medieval romances; while they perhaps did not quite believe in enchanted swords or ogres or flying gryphons, they were not consciously composing fantastic novels. After all, the author of *Amadis of Gaul,* while he had never seen a dragon or visited the country of Prester John, was still a child of his time: if there were no firedrakes or giants in his day, that did not mean they had not abounded in the earlier period in which his tale was set. But Morris was an educated Englishman, consciously concocting an imitation of medieval romance. He knew that dragons were a biological impossibility, but he put them in the story anyway: dragons belong in heroic fantasy.

Morris' novels are immense, sometimes running to two volumes; *The Well at the World's Edge* must total nearly 300,000 words, at a conservative estimate. Epic in scope and concept, written with richness and dignity, they are tales of heroic adventure and mighty deeds which bear a distinct resemblance to Tolkien's trilogy.

THE ARISTOCRAT

When William Morris died in 1896, his direct literary successor, a young Irish nobleman, the Hon. Edward John Moreton Drax Plunkett, was a boy of eighteen. He was descended from one of the oldest baronial houses in the British Isles, heir to a title that stretched back to the Norman Conquest. As Lord Dunsany, the eighteenth baron of his line, he was to become the famous author of many novels, plays, volumes of autobiography, essays, verse, collections of short stories, and a translation of the odes of Horace.

Lord Dunsany was very much the aristocratic Anglo-Irish nobleman, the dedicated sportsman, the titled artist. A tall man (three or four inches over six feet) with an erect, military bearing, he was a graduate of Eton and Sandhurst and served as an officer in the

Coldstream Guards during the Boer War and the First World War. He lived part of the time in a romantic twelfth-century Norman castle in County Meath, Ireland, and part of the time in an old country estate in Kent, England—when he was not in Africa on safari or traveling around the world. He wrote over sixty books in all.

If William Morris was the first writer to fully exploit the potentials of the heroic fantasy, Lord Dunsany was the second. He wrote only a few fantasy novels, of which the finest is *The King of Elfland's Daughter* (1924). Most of his important work in heroic fantasy lies in the field of the short story. His first collection of short fantasies was *The Gods of Pegana* in 1905, swiftly followed by other collections such as *The Book of Wonder, A Dreamer's Tales, Time and the Gods,* and *Tales of Three Hemispheres*. No one with any pretensions toward having a good acquaintanceship with modern fantastic literature can afford to pass them up. Dunsany was not only a born storyteller, but the master as well of a splendid prose style that is a joy to read.

His best fantasies have such titles as "The Fortress Unvanquishable Save for Sacnoth," "The Sword of Welleran," "How One Came, As Was Foretold, to The City of Never," and "The Distressing Tale of Thangobrind the Jeweller." His exquisite little tales, laid in fabulous lands "at the edge of the world" or at least "beyond the fields we know," are drawn from Icelandic saga and medieval romance and are in part inspired by the wonder tales in Herodotus and the Bible.

In "The Fortress Unvanquishable," for example, the young hero Leothric slays a dragon and removes from its body the sword Sacnoth, with which (he is advised by the Magician of Allathurion) the famed citadel of the enchanter may be overwhelmed and taken. In "Carcassonne" the bold, conquering young king, Camorak of Arn, hearing a minstrel's song of a gorgeous city far away, rises up in the night with all his host and marches out to find and possess it. "The Sword of Welleran" tells how the long dead heroes of Merimna —"Welleran, Soorenard, Mommolek, Rollory, Akanax, and young Iraine"—defend their glorious and beloved city against savage tribesmen from beyond the Cyresian mountains. And in "The Hoard of the Gibbelins," the knight Alderic ventures astride a tame dragon beyond the Forest Unpassable to the world's edge, where the incredible treasure lies strangely guarded. But let me give a taste of Dunsany's prose:

> The Gibbelins eat, as is well known, nothing less good than man. Their evil tower is joined to Terra Cognita, to the lands we know, by a bridge. Their hoard is beyond reason; avarice has no use for it; they have a separate cellar for emeralds, and a separate cellar for sapphires; they have filled a hole with gold and dig it up when they need it.

Or this, from "The Bride of the Man-Horse":

> And he took with him too that clarion of the centaurs, that famous silver horn, that in its time had summoned to surrender seventeen cities of Man, and for twenty years had brayed at star-girt walls in the Siege of Tholdenblarna, the citadel of the gods, what time the centaurs waged their fabulous war and were not broken by any force of arms, but retreated slowly . . . before that final miracle of the gods that They brought in Their desperate need from Their ultimate armoury.

A leading contemporary fantasy writer and critic, L. Sprague de Camp, has written that Lord Dunsany probably had the greatest influence on fantasy writers of any writer during the first half of this century. I would say that is an accurate estimate of Dunsany's impact. For he is, far more than Morris, a "writer's writer." Although Dunsany was widely published and reprinted and although his plays were performed at the Abbey Theatre in Dublin and sometimes imported to New York, he did not win a very large readership and never wrote anything remotely resembling a best seller. His singing, crystalline prose, studded with long, curious, magical, and evocative names, and his occasional tendency to allow style to become dominant over plot—these conspired against his chances at wide popularity.

But his influence on the next generation or two of fantasy writers was immense. The American writer H. P. Lovecraft began his apprenticeship as an author by slavishly imitating Dunsany in a number of short stories, such as "Celephais" and "The Doom That Came to Sarnath"; at the conclusion of this period Lovecraft wrote a strange fantasy novel completely in the Dunsanian manner, *The Dream Quest of Unknown Kadath.* Such other fantasy writers as Clark Ashton Smith and Robert E. Howard (the creator of "Conan of Cimmeria" and "King Kull") and Jack Vance show the unmistakable signs of strong Dunsanian influence.

THE ROMANCER

In the year of William Morris' death, when the future Lord Dunsany was a young man of eighteen, another writer was alive who would eventually follow in the tradition of Morris and Dunsany. Eric Rücker Eddison was then a boy of fourteen. Born in 1882 at

Adel, Yorkshire, he became a successful British civil servant in the Board of Trade; from 1930 to 1937 he was Deputy Comptroller-General of the Department of Overseas Trade. But E. R. Eddison had no love for the twentieth century, any more than William Morris had for the nineteenth. His passion lay with the great Norse eddas and sagas, and in 1937, at the age of fifty-five, Eddison retired and devoted the remainder of his life—less than ten years—to creating some of the most remarkable prose romances in the English language.

His first novel, *The Worm Ouroboros,* was written in 1922. It shows his love for the Scandinavian myths and the influence of the sagas, perhaps even the influence of William Morris. It is a magnificent, full-bodied work of heroic adventure laid in a robust, richly colored world of Eddison's imagination, which is vaguely identified with the planet Mercury but we are not intended to take that very seriously.

The plot—the dual themes of quest and war—are very close to Tolkien. The story is about the great war between the lords of Demonland and King Gorice XII of Witchland. Orville Prescott, book critic for *The New York Times,* laid his finger on the book's main flaw when he wrote:

> Since this is a romantic epic about an imaginary world, Eddison felt it necessary to set his stage and explain things before launching into his story proper. This he did awkwardly, by sending an English gentleman in a magic dream to the planet Mercury to observe events there. It is a distracting and clumsy notion; but since Eddison forgot all about his earthborn observer after the first 20 pages, no prospective reader should allow himself to be troubled by his fleeting presence.

143

The main opponents of the sinister and magnificent King Gorice are three brothers, lords of Demonland named Juss, Goldry Bluzco, and Spitfire, and their hellion cousin, Lord Brandoch Daha. Gorice, a potent necromancer, employs his villainous magic and orders the Lord Goldry Bluzco carried off and imprisoned on a great mountain, Koshtra Pivrarcha. His kinsmen embark on a quest to effect his rescue, and the legions of Witchland ravish their realm in their absence.

In a splendid scene, complete with a fascinating battle with a monstrous manticore, the heroes scale the dizzying peaks of Koshtra Pivrarcha and strive for the aid of Queen Sophonisba, "the fosterling of the gods," who has dwelt on Koshtra Belorn for centuries of timeless youth. She tells the Lord Juss that only on hippogriffback can he reach his imprisoned brother. The heroes attempt a rescue anyway; failing, they return again to Demonland, where a hippogriff egg is hidden at the bottom of a lake.

During these adventures King Gorice's merciless lord, Corinius, has marched through their realm with fire and sword. With the aid of a somber, melancholy, and traitorous lord named Gro, their sister Mevrian has narrowly escaped the clutches of Gorice's ruthless captain. The Demon Lords return, drive the warriors of Witchland from their holdings, and accomplish the rescue of Goldry Bluzco. Then the hosts of Demonland bring the war to Gorice and lay siege to his citadel of Carcë. Eventually, in a splendid and vigorous battle which Eddison describes in a superb burst of tempestuous, ringing prose, they overwhelm the lords of Witchland and win a glorious victory.

But victory is hollow. The warrior lords of Demonland are now without adversaries worthy of their heroic manhood and fighting strength. At the very end, therefore, the high gods bestow a mighty miracle upon the heroes: time turns back again, and like the Ouroboros of the title—a serpent devouring its own tail, a circle without beginning or end—the tale begins again.

The pages of Eddison's princely romantic epic are filled with ringing speeches, magnificent passages of description and poetry, glorious scenes of battle and adventure. His characters are truly Homeric, larger than life. As Orville Prescott put it: "In these pages courage and nobility and loyalty are almost taken for granted; women are beautiful and to be served; and glory is worth striving for." Even the villains are magnificent in their villainy.

The Worm was a considerable success for a novel 462 pages long, buttressed with scholarly appendices and chronologies. After its British edition, it was published in New York in 1926, reprinted in hard covers in 1952, and revived in paperback by Ballantine Books in 1967.

Eddison went on to write his Zimiamvian trilogy, comprised of *Mistress of Mistresses* (1935), *A Fish Dinner at Memison* (1941), and *The Mezentian Gate* (1958), *Gate* was left unfinished at Eddison's death in 1945, but those portions of it which he had completed, together with his drafts and rather extensive notes, were assembled into a volume which was issued under that title thirteen years after his death.

The Zimiamvian books are less successful than the mighty *Worm* or, at least, they are less interesting to read. *The Worm* has a swift, direct appeal to the primary emotions: it is concerned with nothing but glorious, stirring adventure. But the Zimiamvian books have a dual theme: they are about adventure but are equally involved in the symbolic presentation of a complex and abstruse philosophy. The *Worm* is a richly colored, thundering tale of battle and quest and heroic derring-do. The trilogy is about political intrigue and politics, plot and counterplot. *The Worm* is Homeric; the trilogy is Machiavellian: and most people enjoy reading Homer more than Machiavelli.

The major character in the trilogy is the goddess Aphrodite, who appears throughout in a number of more or less simultaneous avatars: first as Fiorinda, mistress of the ambitious Duke Barganax; then as Queen Antiope; then as the Duchess of Memison, Barganax' mother; and also as the long-dead wife of the adventurer Lessingham, whom we met briefly in the opening pages of *The Worm*. Another major character is King Mezentius, who plays a leading role in one book and is either off-stage or long-since dead in the others.* He, it turns out, is an avatar of the god Zeus.

Despite these faults, the Zimiamvian trilogy has its admirers. There are many good aspects about it, and some superb fantasy elements. The ambiguous figure of the magician, Dr. Vandermast, provides some beautiful fantasy effects, and the trilogy presents some superb original concepts. For example, the locale is the land of Zimiamvia, which the three lords of Demonland glimpsed dimly from afar when they scaled the heights of Kostra Pivrarcha in *The Worm*. They briefly discuss Zimiamvia in that passage, and it seems that to

---

* Eddison, by the way, borrowed the name of this character from a minor figure in the eighth book of the *Aeneid* of Virgil: the deposed tyrant Mezentius, former king of the Tuscans, who appears leagued with the foes of Aeneas and who is slain in battle against the Trojans in a later book.

the Witches and Demons of Mercury, Zimiamvia is an enchanted or paradisiacal realm.

In the trilogy the reader discovers that Zimiamvia is actually the heaven or Valhalla of the world of *The Worm*. Curiously, Eddison seems to have done very little with this perfectly lovely concept, although early in the trilogy we learn that the goddess Aphrodite permits the dead adventurer, Lessingham, to be reincarnated (or something like that) in this heavenly realm after his death, where he becomes her lover in one of her incarnations. The development is not very easy to make clear and it is less easy to read. Besides, the structure of the trilogy and the relationship of the three novels to one another is confusing; the books are not really sequential. The first two books more or less run parallel to each other, and the unfinished third takes place before the other two.

However, E. R. Eddison was a master of English prose the like of whom has not been seen in our time. After a few pages, I find that my mind simply refuses to try to follow the Machiavellian intricacies of plot and counterplot, stops attempting to figure out which character is which other character's avatar, and simply gets lost in the rich, fine-textured, luxuriant prose, studded with scraps of splendid verse, curious lore of the Middle Ages, odd-sounding names and all manner of oddities, curiosities, and conceits. The following sample is from the scene on the glacier, battling the manticore, in *The Worm*:

> "It hath scented us down the wind," said Brandoch Daha. Small time was there to ponder. Swinging from hold to hold across the dizzy precipice, as an ape swingeth from bough to bough, the beast drew near. The shape of it was as a lion, but bigger and taller, and colour a dull red, and it had prickles lancing out behind, as of a porcupine; its

147

face a man's face, if aught so hideous might be conceived of human kind, with staring eyeballs, low wrinkled brow, elephant ears, some wispy mangy likeness of a lion's mane, huge bony chaps, brown blood-stained gubber-tushes grinning betwixt bristly lips. Straight for the ledge it made, and as they braced them to receive it, with a great swing heaved a man's height above them and leaped down upon their ledge from aloft betwixt Juss and Brandoch Daha ere they were well aware of its changed course. Brandoch Daha smote at it a great swashing blow and cut off its scorpion tail; but it clawed Juss's shoulder, smote down Mivarsh, and charged like a lion upon Brandoch Daha, who, missing his footing on a narrow edge of rock, fell backwards a great fall, clear of the cliff, down to the snow an hundred feet beneath them.

Beyond these four novels, E. R. Eddison also produced a rousing historical novel titled *Styrbiorn the Strong* (1926), the best novel of life in the Viking Age that I have ever found. Eddison drew upon various sources in Scandinavian saga literature, including the William Morris translation of the *Eyrbyggja Saga,* from which he quotes in a prefatory note. Like William Morris, he also did some direct translations, such as his version of *Egil's Saga.*

Eddison had a profound influence on later fantasy writers and won many ardent supporters. Anthony Boucher and Orville Prescott admired *The Worm* greatly. Fantasy novelists like James Stephens and James Branch Cabell and even C. S. Lewis praised it in extravagant terms.

The American historian of the Civil War and naval events Fletcher Pratt (1897–1956) was an enthusiastic admirer of Eddison and learned much from him. In collaboration with L. Sprague de Camp in the 1940's, Pratt wrote such novels of fantasy adventure as *Land of Unreason* and *The Carnelian Cube* and a trilogy about the adventures of a young American scientist named

Harold Shea, who ventures into the worlds of Norse myth, Irish legend, the Finnish *Kalevala,* Ariosto's *Orlando,* and other realms of imagination. On his own, Pratt authored two brilliant minor classics in the genre of the epic fantasy. The first and finest of these, *The Well of the Unicorn* (1948), clearly shows the unambiguous influences of William Morris (from whom Pratt borrowed the names of some characters and probably the concept of "the Well"), E. R. Eddison (his world is a sort of medieval Scandinavian one, written in saga-like prose), and Lord Dunsany.* The second of these, *The Blue Star* (1952), eschews the heroics and battle pieces of the first and is laid in a very intriguing world akin to the eighteenth-century Austrian empire of Maria Theresa.

Then there is Mervyn Peake. Without a note on his remarkable Gormenghast trilogy this chapter would be severely lacking. For although not truly in the same line of literary descent as Tolkien's work, his trilogy is comparable to *The Lord of the Rings* in its rich imaginative fertility, scope, depth, and range, if not for its mastery of prose.

Mervyn Laurence Peake, a British poet, playwright, novelist, and illustrator (of *Treasure Island,* the Brothers Grimm, and, happily, of his own books) wrote an astounding and terrifying and beautiful novel called *Titus Groan,* which the British firm of Eyre & Spottiswoode first published in 1946. On a mist-shrouded world, bleak and barren and desolate, with endless moors, rises the eons-old and inconceivably immense castle of Gormenghast, a vast, intricate, sprawling, de-

---

* In a preface Pratt explains that his is the world of Lord Dunsany's play *King Argimenes and the Unknown Warrior* but laid some generations later.

caying edifice which is, so far as the novel tells us, the only thing on all its nameless, darkling planet. Therein, for thousands of years, have ruled the Earls of Gormenghast. The character for whom the novel was named, Titus himself, will someday become the seventy-seventh earl of this enormous, rotting pile of ancient masonry. He is only an infant throughout the bulk of the first volume.

What Mervyn Peake has done is to construct a closed world, a world in miniature, and to explore the roots of human character through the knotted, tangled, intricately interwoven lives of the scores of odd, deformed, subtle, monstrous, robust, or decadent creatures who inhabit the gigantic castle. He tells no real story but explores the ways in which characters interact with each other. His nightmarish castle, with its cobwebbed and crumbling maze of corridors and musty suites, with its weird cast of human oddities, its complex network of social customs, forms the setting for a dark, dramatic, complex narrative that holds the reader enthralled and spellbound.

A sequel, *Gormenghast,* followed in 1950, and a rather unsatisfactory third novel completed the trilogy in 1959; it was called *Titus Alone.*

Peake is the literary heir perhaps of the Brontës, with their foggy moors and stormy passions; certainly of Kafka, as a glance at *The Castle* demonstrates. The rich, fecund texture of his prose and his hothouse-orchid setting in surroundings of rotting baronial magnificence fallen to squalor and neglect, together with the malevolence and grotesqueries of his characters, hearken back to the old Gothic tradition, although this work is no *Dracula.* But he is strongly Dickensian, as well, in the fertility and gusto and power of his dense, darkling prose. In a word, the Gormenghast trilogy defies easy comparison and must be read. Ballantine Books has brought the entire trilogy into print in this country for the first time.

Together, William Morris, Lord Dunsany, Eric Rücker Eddison, and the writers whom they influenced and continue to influence created the tradition of the epic, heroic fantasy romance—the precise tradition to which *The Lord of the Rings* belongs in every way. When William Morris died in 1896, Lord Dunsany was a young man of eighteen, E. R. Eddison was a youth of fourteen, and J. R. R. Tolkien was a child of four.

Now that the descent of the epic fantasy tradition from the classic epic and the *chanson de geste* to the medieval romance and the fantasy novel has been clarified, this study can turn to Professor Tolkien and trace the ways in which he appears to have made use of this tradition.

14.

Tolkien's Basic Sources

~~~~~~

THE ELDER EDDA

About ten years ago, in late 1959, I stumbled by accident upon the first major source Professor Tolkien had employed in creating his Middle-earth mythos.

At this time, only three years after the first hardcover edition of *The Lord of the Rings* had been published in the United States, the trilogy was still largely unknown—at least to the general reading public, although it had already been discovered by a small hardcore readership made up of enthusiasts of heroic fantasy, such as myself. But very little of a serious critical nature had yet been published on the trilogy or its author—one of the few exceptions being Edmund Wilson's major essay in *The Nation,* which was very negative. The paperbound editions were yet to popularize Tolkien and his work. We were still some six years away from the first mass-circulation printings and the tremendous broad-spectrum readership they were to win for the trilogy.

I was at the time searching through *The Elder Edda,* tracking down a certain verse that I remembered vaguely, as I wanted to quote the correct text of this verse as a chapter heading in a fantasy novel I was then writing.

The Elder Edda is, to me, one of the most fascinating books in the world. I had discovered it years earlier and had twice read it in its entirety—but that was long before I had read *The Hobbit* or even heard of Tolkien. Some of the excitement of my discovery will be clear if the Dwarf names Tolkien mentions—such as Durin, Dwalin, Dain, Bifur, Bofur, Bombur, Nori, Thrain, Thorin, Thror, Fíli, Kíli, Fundin, Glóin, Dori, Ori—are kept in mind. Hunting for the verse I remembered, I leafed through the opening book of *The Elder Edda*— and was stopped cold at stanza 10.

9. Then sought the gods   their assembly-seats
      The holy ones,   and council held,
   To find who should raise   the race of dwarfs,
      Out of Brimir's blood   and the legs of Blain.

---

* My copy of *The Elder Edda,* and the edition which I used and referred to in this present work, is called *The Poetic Edda* (an alternate title—it is also sometimes mentioned by scholars under the title of *Edda Saemundar;* I happen to prefer the *Elder Edda* title and have used it throughout). In a translation by Henry Adams Bellows, it forms volumes XXI and XXII of the Scandinavian Classics series, published by The American-Scandinavian Foundation, New York; fourth printing, 1957. Incidentally, Tolkien enthusiasts who may be inspired by this chapter to search out the *Voluspo* for careful reading will perhaps be interested to learn that no less a dedicated Tolkienist than Mr. W. H. Auden has recently completed a new verse translation of this, the first book of the *Edda.* Mr. Auden plans to render other selections from the *Edda* into English verse for a forthcoming book.

10. There was Motsognir   the mightiest made
    Of all the dwarfs,   and *Durin* next;
    Many a likeness   of men they made,
The dwarfs in the earth,   as Durin said.

11.   Nyi and Nithri,   Northri and Suthri,
    Austri and Vestri,   Althjof, *Dvalin,*
    Nar and Nain,   Niping, *Dain,*
    Bifur, Bofur,   *Bombur, Nori,*
    An and Onar,   Ai, Mjothvitnir.

12. Vigg and Gandalf (!)   Vindalf, *Thrain,*
    Thekk and *Thorin,*   *Thror,* Vit and Lit,
    Nyr and Nyrath—   now have I told—
    Regin and Rathsvith—   the list aright.

13.   *Fili, Kili,*   *Fundin,* Nali,
    Heptifili,   Hannar, Sviur,
    Frar, Hornbori,   Fraeg and Loni,
    Aurvang, Jari,   Eikinskjaldi.

14. The race of the dwarfs   in Dvalin's throng
    Down to Lofar   the list must I tell;
    The rocks they left,   and through wet lands
    They sought a home   in the fields of sand.

15. There were Draupnir   and Dolgthrasir,
    Hor, Haugspori,   Hlevang, *Gloin,*
    Dori, Ori,   Duf, Andvari,
    Skirfir, Virfir,   Skafith, Ai.

There, from just six verses, Tolkien borrowed the names for sixteen of his Dwarves—to say nothing of Gandalf himself, who appears in the *Edda* listed among the dwarves (a footnote defines his name as meaning "magic elf," and it has been suggested that the Eddaic Gandalf is supposed to be a half-breed, a mixture of elf and dwarf).

I became so interested in my discovery that I sat down, with the *Edda* and the Tolkien books open in front of me, and started on the pleasant game of name hunting. I soon turned up another "find." The dwarf

Thorin in the *Edda* appears in Tolkien as Thorin Oakenshield. I found that the name of the dwarf Eikin-
skjaldi, mentioned in the last line of Stanza 13 quoted
above, means "oaken-shield" in the original Old Norse.
Hence Tolkien combined the names of two dwarves
into one to create his character. My research led me
into other books and to further discoveries, most of
which I put together into a long essay, "Notes on
Tolkien," which was serialized in the magazine *Xero*.*

The dwarf names which Tolkien borrowed appear in a long cosmological and prophetic poem, *Voluspo*, or "Song of the Wise Woman," which is the first
book of *The Elder Edda*. The Edda is a very ancient
work of Norse literature—it could be called the Old
Testament of Norse mythology. Like the Old Testament, to which it may be said to have close structural
resemblance, the *Edda* is a huge, haphazard anthology
of some thirty-five books, most in verse but some in
prose; it is a miscellaneous collection of history, heroic
legend, poetry, proverbs, religious myths, genealogy,
pure fable, theology, and cosmogony. *The Elder Edda*
is the original source, the fountainhead, of Norse mythology. Every Norse myth in modern literature, in
every version or form, from L. Sprague de Camp and
Fletcher Pratt's Harold Shea story, "The Roaring
Trumpet" in *The Incomplete Enchanter* all the way to
Richard Wagner's *Ring* cycle of operas, springs from
this one work.

---

* The first installment of "Notes on Tolkien" appeared in the issue
dated November, 1961, and the conclusion of the serialized essay
was printed in the September, 1962, issue. A greatly condensed version of the same basic series of articles was printed in *Triumph*
magazine under the title "What About This Tolkien Fellow, Anyway?" in the issue for November, 1966.

No one knows how old these stories are; so far as modern scholarship knows they were first written down in Iceland, then a Norse colony, probably in the middle of the thirteenth century A.D. The only surviving manuscript was and is now preserved in the Royal Library at Copenhagen as *Codex Regius*. But the stories are far older than Saemund's time. In oral form they may date back to the days of the great "Aryan migration"—that nebulous and inadequately documented period when the forefathers of the Northern peoples were scattered nomadic tribes wandering the face of Europe; this spread is referred to by German historians as the *Völkerwanderung,* the Migrations of Nations of the Dark Ages. Out of these epic migrations and adventures arose legends and heroes whose tales were handed down and embellished by generations of story tellers among the ancestors of the Norse and Germanic peoples in the dark confusion of the days before they settled down in the Scandinavian peninsula.

As I searched through the other books of *The Elder Edda* I found that Tolkien had borrowed much from the entire corpus of Norse myth, and my curiosity led me to explore the other, later works of Norse or Germanic literature to see if Tolkien had found anything there to use. He had. My discovery was a legitimate one, independent of other writings about Tolkien and his sources. I was still years from reading Henry Resnik's *Saturday Evening Post* article referred to earlier in this book, and such insights as:

Tolkien's long acquaintance with Norse and Germanic myths has inspired the chiller, more menacing landscapes of Middle-earth, and he makes no secret of having deliberately shaped the two major interests of his life—rural England and the northern myths—to his own literary purposes. "In *The Lord of the Rings*," Tolkien says, "I have tried to modernize the myths and make them credible.

"I have tried to modernize the myths": it was not many months before I began to understand exactly what Tolkien had done. Of course any literate person who reads *LOTR* will realize that the author is using certain familiar concepts from general European folklore, literature, and myth. That is, elves, dragons, trolls, and dwarves—all of which are in Tolkien—can also be found in the tales of Grimm and Andersen: Tolkien did not invent them, he used them. But little else in the trilogy looks familiar at first glance. It is not until one takes a long, thoughtful, close look that one begins to see how Tolkien has drawn upon the old Norse and Germanic body of myths and tales and has reshaped their substance to his own purpose.

THE SIEGFRIED LEGEND

One of the greatest stories in *The Elder Edda* is the legend of Siegfried the Dragon-Slayer, who took the fabulous Nibelungen hoard. It is one of the world's greatest stories, comparable to the Arthur-Guinevere-Lancelot tale or the Trojan War. It passed from the *Edda* through a half-dozen later versions and retellings, but in the original it took this form: Sigurth the Volsung slays Fafnir the Dragon and takes the hoard, or treasure, of the evil dwarf, Andvari. He arouses Sigrfrida the Valkyrie from her magical sleep and woos her for King Gunnar, whose wife she becomes. Gunnar, in reward, gives Sigurth Guthrun to wife. Later, Gunnar and Hogni slay Sigurth for the Hoard of the Nibelungs.

This first version of the tale presents the main elements which are to reappear in version after version— elements Tolkien was to draw upon. For example, among Andvari's treasure are "rings of gold," and the dying Dragon prophesies to his slayer, Sigurth (in *Fafnismol,* 20): "And the rings thy bane shall be." Later in the story, as related in *Guthrunarkvitha,* 20, Guthrun, weeping over the corpse of her husband, Sigurth, says:

> "Gunnar, no joy
> the gold shall give thee,
> The rings shall soon
> thy slayers be."

This is the seed from which grew the concept of the magical golden ring that proved the bane of him who possessed it.

As the tale of the Dragon-Slayer passed on, it changed and developed. In the thirteenth century, Snorri Sturluson composed a retelling of *The Elder Edda* which is sometimes called *The Younger Edda,* or *The Prose Edda.* This Snorri, the son of a turbulent and ambitious Icelandic chieftain, himself seems to have been a thoroughly unlikeable sort who sacrificed his friends, relatives, and even his children to his own insatiable ambition. His life, a grim chronicle of avarice, betrayal, and sordid political chicanery, ended in 1241 when he was murdered by his own son-in-law. His *Prose Edda,* however, is a stylistic masterpiece, albeit a puzzling and confused work which attempts to retell the Nordic myths, garnished with scraps of Old Testament legend and linked up uncertainly with the Trojan legend cycle (i.e. the Norse god Odin is depicted as the grandson of King Priam, and so on).

In Snorri's version of the Dragon-Slayer legend, *The Elder Edda's* Sigurth is called Sigurd, and the other characters in the story appear under slightly different names. This abbreviated version of the Eddic tale is given in a section of *The Prose Edda* called the *Skáldskaparmál* (the "Poetry of the Skalds"). Incidentally, our same catalogue of dwarves is quoted directly in Snorri in an earlier book, *Gylfaginning,* 14. *The Prose Edda* is preserved in several old manuscripts; one, which may be a direct copy of Snorri's original manuscript, is in the library of the University of Uppsala (the *Codex Upsaliensis,* dated about 1320 A.D.).

About thirty years after Snorri was assassinated by his son-in-law, the *Volsunga Saga* appeared. Written about 1270 by an anonymous Icelandic poet, it is a re-creation in prose of the stories from *The Elder Edda,* and the unknown author must have worked from a more complete text of the original *Edda* than we possess, for the somewhat fragmentary version is here fleshed out in a tight, continuous narrative. In this version, Sigurd Fafnirsbane inherits the broken sword, which is mended by the dwarf blacksmith, Regin, and called Gram. With it, Sigurd slays the dragon Fafnir and takes the treasure. But he mistrusts Regin, who plans to betray him, and slays him. He rouses Brynhild, the Valkyrie, from her magic sleep and plights troth with her before leaving. Losing all memory of Brynhild through a magic potion, he weds Gunnar's sister, Gudrun, and assists Gunnar to win the Valkyrie, which eventually brings doom down upon him and the others.

Yet another version of the tale appears in the great Anglo-Saxon epic *Beowulf,* in greatly digested form. After Beowulf slays the monster Grendel, a chieftain hails his deed and sings an old song about another monster-killing hero in flattering comparison. In *Beowulf,* Sigurth-Sigurd is called Sigmund, and a ballad version of the slaying of Fafnir is given in *Beowulf,* 13. As we shall see, Tolkien found several useful elements in *Beowulf.*

The mighty German national epic, the *Nibelungenlied,* gives us the legend in nearly its final form. Here is how the German epic tells the tale: Siegfried hears of Kriemhild's beauty and rides to woo her at Worms. He kills the two Nibelungs, Schilbung and Nibelung, and seizes their golden treasure, and from the dwarf, Albric, he takes the Tarnkappe, the Helm of Invisibility. He also slays a dragon and, bathing in its blood, becomes invulnerable to any weapon, save in one spot between his shoulders, where a linden leaf stuck, keeping the dragon blood from rendering that part of his body impervious (much as the Greek hero Achilles was dunked in the waters of the Styx and became invulnerable in every part of his body except for the heel, by which his mother had held him when she did the dunking—had the old Germanic poets possibly read the *Iliad?*). Günther, King of Worms, and the plotter Hagen persuade the invulnerable hero to woo Brünhilde the Valkyrie for the King's bride. He does and weds Kriemhild while Günther marries Brünhilde. The queens quarrel, and Siegfried is murdered by Günther and Hagen at the instigation of Brünhilde, who has discovered the one unprotected spot on his body. Kriemhild inherits the Nibelungen hoard and later marries Etzel, whom she persuades to lure King Günther and Hagen to his kingdom. When they arrive, she traps and kills them, thus revenging the murder of Siegfried.

160

Thus far in the evolution of the story, several of the elements Tolkien was to use have already emerged: the slaying of a dragon, the curse on the dragon's treasure which brings doom to everyone who possesses it, the notion of the talisman of invisibility, and so on. But the tale has one more final stage of development through which to pass.

When Richard Wagner began the composition of his cycle of operas, *The Ring of the Nibelungen,* around 1850, he went straight to this national epic of Germany on the advice of his good friend Franz Liszt. Wagner's stupendous tetralogy was shaped directly from the materials of the epic myth, with, however, some changes that were Wagner's own contribution. What he was trying to do was to reconcile the various conflicting elements in the *Nibelungenlied* and the *Volsunga Saga;* to do this, he had to rewrite the whole story. However, Wagner was a master in his own right, working with the materials of a magnificent tale, and under his gifted hands the story received its final form.

The complete libretti of the *Ring* cycle were first published in 1863, and the cycle itself was first performed in its entirety at Beyreuth from August 13 to August 17, 1876. After more than a thousand years, the legend of the Dragon-Slayer had achieved its ultimate form. Wagner's plot is this:

In *Das Rheingold,* Alberich the Dwarf learns from the Rhine Maidens that the piece of gold they guard at the bottom of the river, if ever it be fashioned into a gold ring, will impart great magical powers to its possessor. Angered when the Rhine Maidens elude his lustful grasp, he seizes the gold and forces the Dwarf Smith, Mime, to fashion it into a ring of power.

Meanwhile Wotan (the Norse Odin in Teutonic

form), King of the Gods, persuades the two Giants, Fasolt and Fafner, to build Valhalla for him, promising that as payment they will receive the Goddess Freia. When they complete the job, Loge the Cunning, by playing upon the greed of the simple Giants, glibly talks them into taking the Ring instead. He says:

> "It gives, when to golden
> Ring is is rounded,
> Power and might unmatched;
> It wins its owner the world."

The Giants agree to this change, whereupon Wotan and Loge visit Alberich, who has now made himself King of the Dwarves by the power of the Ring. They trick him into demonstrating the shape-changing magic of the Ring and capture him in his toad form, forcing him to surrender the Ring, as well as the Tarnhelm of Invisibility and the golden hoard of the dwarves. He does so, but unwillingly, and places this curse on the magic Ring:

> "As a curse gave me the ring,
> My curse go with the ring!
> As its gold
> Gave measureless might,
> May now its magic
> Deal death evermore!"

The Gods then turn over the treasures to the Giants, although Wotan has begun to fall under the curse of the Ring and is loath to surrender it. Then the two Giants, also feeling the deadly curse, quarrel over who shall possess the Ring and battle for it. Fafner kills his brother Fasolt and takes it.

In the third part of Wagner's tetralogy, *Siegfried,*

Mime attempts to mend the broken sword Nothung for the youth Siegfried, but he fails, whereupon Siegfried welds the halves of the broken sword together himself. Armed with Nothung, Siegfried slays Fafner, who has assumed the dragon shape; he does not attempt to slay him through his heavy scales but strikes through his soft, unprotected breast.

Accidentally tasting the dragon's hot blood, Siegfried discovers he can now understand the language of the birds. He overhears the birds, who had watched the slaying of Fafner, say that Siegfried should go into the cave and find the Tarnhelm and the magic Ring itself.

While Siegfried is in the cavern taking the Nibelung-Hoard and the two magic treasures, Alberich and Mime reach the cave, see the dragon is slain, quarrel about which of them should have the Ring, and come near to killing each other. Alberich flees when Siegfried reappears with the loot. Mime tries to get the Ring from the hero, assaults him, and is killed by Siegfried. Siegfried then rescues the Valkyrie, Brünhilde, from her castle surrounded by magic fire, and the great story spins itself out to its conclusion.

ELEMENTS OF THE SIEGFRIED STORY
IN THE TOLKIEN TRILOGY

In the Siegfried legend, as it reached its final form under the hands of Richard Wagner, a certain number of plot elements attract our attention. Among them are these:

1. The dragon guarding a treasure

2. The magic gold ring, which gives its bearer great power but which carries with it a deadly curse

3. A talisman of invisibility which is associated with the treasure

4. The slaying of the dragon through an unprotected spot in its breast

5. The broken sword which is made whole again

6. The quarrel of two dwarves, or two giants, for possession of the Ring, which results in the murder of one of them

7. The wicked little dwarf who possessed the Ring is maddened and perverted by it, and is eventually killed because of it

8. The fact that the Curse of the Ring brings not only death, but a sort of moral decay or greed for possession to all who bear it.

Any reader who has followed my plot outline of *The Lord of the Rings* and *The Hobbit* will swiftly see that all eight of these plot elements are present in Tolkien's narrative. True, he has combined the magic Ring and the Helmet of Invisibility onto a single talisman, but this is his only significant departure from the Siegfried elements. In *The Hobbit,* the dragon Smaug is slain, like Fafner, through an unprotected place in its chest. In *LOTR* the story of The Sword That Was Broken and Is Made Whole occurs when Aragorn reveals that he guards the broken sword of Elendil, Narsil, which is repaired and made whole again and receives the new name, Andúril, "Flame of the West." Tolkien uses the scene in which the hero learns the speech of birds and receives wise advice from one. In Chapter XV of *The Hobbit* the raven Roac, son of

Carc, brings word to Thorin Oakenshield that Smaug is slain. Tolkien also duplicates the scene in which the two little dwarves, Alberich and Mime, struggle for possession of the Ring and one of them is slain; for Gollum got the Ring in the first place, when his name was Sméagol, and he fought with and murdered his brother Déagol to keep it. Even the detail of Wotan the All-Father, who, although he is King of the Gods, yet feels the irresistible lure of the Ring, is repeated in the trilogy when Gandalf the mighty magician refuses to take up the burden of the Ring "because even he might be tempted to use it."

There can be little reason to doubt that Professor Tolkien had studied the Siegfried legend in each of its major retellings described above. We know this because he uses facets or ideas or elements which in some cases are peculiar only to one single version of the legend. For example, the fight between Mime and Alberich for the Ring is found in that form only in Wagner. The catalogue of dwarf names in the Edda is not found in Wagner, and he must therefore have studied both of these sources. The names from Beowulf appear in that poem alone.

15.

On the Naming of Names

Then sought the gods   their assembly-seats,
    The holy ones,   and council held;
Names then gave they   to noon and twilight,
Morning they named,   and the waning moon,
    Night and evening,   the years to number.
The Elder Edda, Voluspo, 6

When I discovered that Professor Tolkien had used the famous catalogue of dwarf names from the first book of *The Elder Edda* as a source for the names of some of his characters, I did not at first realize that the borrowing went further.

Such references are not particularly unusual. Many writers of fantasy and other works make use of the necessity to invent new names for their stories to play little personal jokes for the amusement of their friends or fellow writers. The well-known American writer of Poe-style horror tales, H. P. Lovecraft, frequently employed this device. For example, he used a little-known fact about the family history of his friend and correspondent, the writer August W. Derleth, and made a small, private in-joke when he listed the imaginary author of one of the invented tomes of eldrich lore mentioned in some of his stories as "the Comte d'Erlette."

The joke involved is more than just the obvious pun on the similarity in sound between "Derleth" and "d'Erlette," but few readers outside of Lovecraft's circle of intimates could be expected to know that Derleth is descended from French nobility, that the original family name, d'Erlette, was changed to Derleth as a result of the family's flight from France to Bavaria during the French Revolution, and that the title, Comte, was hereditary in the line until that point in its history. I did not know this myself until August Derleth explained it to me. As an American citizen, of course, Mr. Derleth cannot retain a title of nobility.

Lovecraft played the same sort of joke on himself in some of his other stories, using an old family name, Ward Phillips, as another of his imaginary authors of some loathly text of nameless lore or other. One of his correspondents played a comparable joke on him; as a young *Weird Tales* writer at the beginning of his career, many years before he was to become known as the author of *Psycho* and many other books and movies, Robert Bloch wrote a story in H. P. L.'s "Cthulhu Mythos" called *The Suicide in the Study*. In it, he has reference to a loathsome text of primal sorcery written by "the mad Luveh-Keraphf, priest of Bast"—Luveh-Keraphf-Lovecraft, an overobvious pun.*

I presumed that Tolkien was no more immune to this sort of temptation than any other writer. Besides personal in-jokes, the more scholarly authors of fantastic fiction are sometimes given to using their special-

---

* Perhaps inspired by Lovecraft's frequent mention of "the Commorium myth-cycle, preserved by the Atlantean high-priest, Klarkash-ton," which is a joke on a series of stories about Hyperborea written by Lovecraft's friend, the late Californian poet, sculptor, author, and artist Clark Ashton Smith.

ized knowledge in their books in the same way Tolkien used dwarf names from the *Edda* for his own Dwarf characters. Similarly, C. S. Lewis in his brilliant "Narnia" books gave the name of his wonderful lion-god as "Aslan"—the Persian word for "lion" is *arslan*.

I assumed Tolkien to be doing what had been done before by other authors. The very popular and prolific American science fiction and fantasy writer, Poul Anderson, who is of Danish descent, drew upon the materials of Norse saga and myth for the background lore of his excellent fantasy novel *The Broken Sword,* which was published by Abelard-Schuman in 1959, about the same time that the first edition of the first volume of Tolkien's trilogy was being printed in Great Britain. *The Broken Sword* is the story of a mortal boy taken as changeling by Imric the elf-earl and raised in Faerie. In the story Mr. Anderson uses many elements from the body of Northern myth we have just been discussing the sources of *LOTR:* the Tarnkappe in the story; are some dwarves from the *Voluspo* catalogue (including "Dyrin"—Tolkien called him "Durin"—and Dvalin), trolls, dwarves, elves, dragons, and the concept of the broken sword itself. This does not, of course, mean that Poul Anderson borrowed these elements from Tolkien: that would be impossible, because of the dates alone, since *The Broken Sword* was probably written a year or more before its publication, and hence was conceived before any portion of the trilogy had been printed. It simply means that Poul Anderson borrowed from the same Icelandic sources from which the Professor also borrowed.

As I delved further into the problem of Tolkien's sources, I found many more evidences that he had used the *Edda* for more than merely his dwarf names.

For example, the dark, enchanted forest Mirkwood is mentioned many times in the *Edda*. In *Lokasenna*, the eighth book of *The Elder Edda*, stanza 42, we find:

> But when Muspell's sons through Myrkwood ride,
> Thou shalt weaponless wait, poor wretch.

The first stanza of the *Volundarkvitha*, the fifteenth book of the *Edda*, has this:

> Maids from the south through Myrkwood flew,
>   Fair and young, their fate to follow

All in all, Mirkwood is mentioned some seventeen times in the *Edda*, and the notes to my edition explain the term as "a stock name for a dark, gloomy, magical forest."

As Michael Straight observed in his article "The Fantastic World of Professor Tolkien," * Tolkien prepared himself for the task of creating his Middle-earth mythos by "immersion in Welsh, Norse, Gaelic, Scandinavian and Germanic folklore"; in short, he steeped himself in the elements and materials that are part of the common European heritage of tradition, language, literature, culture, and beliefs. This remark proved true enough, for as I began exploring sources other than the great *Edda*, I found elements used by Tolkien everywhere.

The dwarf Thrain appears (as a Viking king of Valland), for example, in the saga of Hromund Greipsson, where he battles mightily with the magic sword, Mistilteinn. Armed with the enchanted blade, he could not be slain while he bore it, and by the time the wily

---

* *The New Republic*, January 16, 1956.

Hromond takes it from him by guile, he has already slaughtered 144 warriors. Durin and Dvalin also appear in the saga of Hervör and Heithrek, where the god Odin forces them to forge the mythic sword, Tyrfing, for Odin's grandson, King Svafrlame. Compelled against their will to perform this odious task, the spiteful dwarves pronounce a dreadful curse over the enchanted blade, to the effect that it should never thenceafter be drawn from its sheath without causing a man's death. Durin and Dvalin turn up again, later, this time in the saga of King Heidrek the Wise, and so does Mirkwood. Mirkwood is mentioned in almost every source,* even in William Morris' novel, *The House of the Wulfings*.

Gandalf is fairly popular, too. His first appearance is in the *Edda*'s dwarf catalogue, where he seems to be a sort of dwarf-elf halfbreed. But another "Gandalf" plays a minor role in a fourteenth-century Norse saga, the *Tháttr Nornagest Saga* (see N. Kershaw: *Stories and Ballads of the Far Past*, Cambridge, 1921). And, to confuse matters even more, a character called "Gandolf [*sic*] the Bear" has a small part in William Morris' novel, *The Well at the World's End,* in Chapter Two, Book IV.

The two characters who led me the merriest chase, and gave me the most fun in tracing their derivations, were Eärendil and Frodo himself.

Eärendil, who does not appear on stage in Tolkien, is an ancient hero of the elves; Aragorn tells the Hob-

---

* For that matter, so is Durin. He even makes an appearance in the Portuguese romance *Amadis of Gaul,* but as a wandering knight called "Durin of Denmark," not as a dwarf.

bits something about him in the first book, Chapter 11: "Elwing the White whom Eärendil wedded, he that sailed his ship out of the mists of the world into the seas of heaven with the Silmaril upon his brow. And of Eärendil came the Kings of Númenor, that is Westernesse." Tolkien tells us more about him in Appendix A, I(i). With the power of the *silmaril* he passed into the Uttermost West, where, speaking as both ambassador of Elves and Men, he obtained the aid of greater ones, by whose power Morgoth was overthrown. But "Eärendil was not permitted to return to mortal lands, and his ship bearing the *silmaril* was set to sail in the heavens as a star, and a sign of hope to the dwellers in Middle-earth oppressed by the Great Enemy or his servants." "Eärendil the Mariner," the elves call him. He is not a very important figure in *The Lord of the Rings* (although he may well prove a major character in *The Silmarillion* when that prequel to the trilogy finally reaches print).

Thus Eärendil became a star. It happens that—according to Viktor Rydberg, an early authority on Teutonic myth—one of the very few Teutonic star names we know is *Earendel,* or *Orvandel,* identified as the Morning Star (the planet Venus) and called by these names by the descendents of the Saxons in Britain. Tracing the story of Earendel-Orvandel back to *The Prose Edda,* we find that Orvandel—or Orwandel, as it is called in this tale—figures in an amusing anecdote concerning one of Thor's expeditions into Jotunheim. He is a big, brave hunter, husband of the witch Groa, father of the hero Swipdag, enemy of the giant Coller and the monster Sela, a famous giant fighter and friend of the god Thor, whom he met while Thor was on his way to giant-land and helped Orwandel cross a river by putting him in a basket and carrying him over. The only portion of Orwandel's anatomy which was exposed to the frigid air of Jotunheim was his big toe, which stuck out of the basket. When it froze solid, the helpful Thor snapped it off and, to honor the stoical hero who had not winced or cried aloud, Thor threw it up in the heavens, where it became a star appropriately called "Orwandel's Toe." This name was later shortened to "Orvandel." Later, when the Saxons were converted to Christianity (Rydberg reports with a straight face), they came to regard this star as a symbol of Christ, and Orvandel, or Earendel, gradually became in Old English an abstract word meaning "splendor." The *Codex Exoniensis* preserves a scrap of an ancient hymn which uses this symbolism:

> Eala Earendel
> engla beorhtast
> ofer Middangeard
> monnum sended

Which means:

> O Orvandel
> brightest shining of angels
> thou who over Middle-Earth
> art sent to men.*

To this point the matter of Eärendil is an interesting bit of lore, illustrating the way Tolkien seized upon an old Germanic star name which became identified as a symbol of the Savior and also an angel and turned it into an Elvish savior-hero. But the story does not end here. I did a little more checking and found that Or-

---

* See Viktor Rydberg, *Teutonic Mythology*, vol. 3, pp. 768–769.

vandel can be traced back beyond *The Prose Edda;* as a great archer and star-hero, he is a universal divinity of ancient Aryan origin. He appears in Greek mythology as the divine hunter, Orion; under another slight name change, he also has a place in such Hindu mythological epics as the *Rig-Veda*. And—moving forward in time from *The Prose Edda*—he became a popular figure in Scandinavian story telling long after Snorri.

He can be found, for example, in the work of Saxo Grammaticus, who is not only the earliest Danish historian, but is considered one of the most notable historians of the Middle Ages. He lived about A.D. 1150 to around 1200, and wrote a history of his country, the celebrated (and very readable) *Gesta Danorum*. The first nine books of Saxo's history incorporate tales and traditions of the kings and heroes up to about the year 950, and this is the section that concerns us. The *Gesta Danorum* is still important, in part because it is the source from which Shakespeare borrowed the plot of Hamlet. In the original story as told by Saxo Grammaticus, Hamlet appears as "Prince Amleth," and his murdered father is none other than our old friend, Orvandel, here known as Horwendil. Thus if you like, you can trace a direct link between *The Lord of the Rings, Hamlet,* the Sanskrit *Rig-Veda,* and the Greek myth of Orion.

There is one further step. For as "Horvendillus" Orvandel passed into medieval romances, from which the recent American novelist, James Branch Cabell, borrowed him. Cabell (1879–1958) is best known to the general reading public as the author of *Jurgen* (1919), which was roundly condemned as salacious by John S. Sumner's American Society for the Suppression of

Vice and became a famous *cause célèbre* to rank with *Ulysses, Tropic of Cancer,* and other suppressed books. But Cabell wrote more than fifty books besides *Jurgen,* which, although the best-known of his novels (and, rather sadly, the only one still in print), is no more entertaining than certain other of his erudite, urbane, polished, and witty fantasy novels, such as *The High Place, The Silver Stallion, Something About Eve,* and my own personal favorite, *The Cream of the Jest.*

Most of Cabell's works are linked into a giant super-novel called *Biography of Manuel.* In it, Cabell constructed an amazingly complicated universe, with very involved chains of command of spiritual hierarchies (the Judeo-Christian God, for example, has a place in it, but only because Jurgen's grandmother raised such a stink upon dying and not finding herself in the sort of afterworld so meticulously depicted in Revelations that Koschei the Deathless was forced to invent Him in order to shut her up). It is sometimes difficult to recognize who is top dog in Cabell's cosmos, but it is most often the dream-self of novelist Felix Kennaston (who stands for Cabell himself). Using a magic talisman called the Sigil of Scoteia, Kennaston in his dreams becomes the "wandering demiurge" Horvendile, who is simultaneously making up the stories Kennaston will later write and also playing a role (usually an ambiguous and background part) in the stories as they take place. Horvendile appears in several of the books of the *Biography,* but he is the major character in *The Cream of the Jest.*

Cabell may have encountered the name "Horvendillus" in the later French courtly romances, or "Horwendil" in the *Gesta Danorum.* Cabell is one of the most erudite of all the fantasy writers thus far discussed, and Saxo Grammaticus is just the sort of literary oddity he would have read. But from whatever source he first took Horvendile, he went on to explore the sources mentioned, and he seems to have traced the ubiquitous Orion-Orvandel-Earendil-Horvendillus through his many incarnations.* From whatever source he hails, Horvendile went straight to the center of Cabell's cosmos. And thereby Cabell set a mystery for his readers. He could not at this date have known that many years afterward, having completed the *Biography,* he would turn to lesser books such as *Hamlet Had an Uncle* (1940). His intention was to turn to Saxo Grammaticus and retell the story of Hamlet as Saxo did it—that is, as a sort of Viking saga, ignoring what Shakespeare added to the original plot.† Of course he was forced to use the name Horvendile, which is used in Saxo for Hamlet's father. This double use of one name must have caused no end of puzzlement to Cabell fans who were at a loss to find some hidden meaning in this coincidence and to establish a connection between this novel and the *Biography.*

---

* Cabell himself shrewdly inserts the Welsh "Morning Star" lore in one of the romances in the *Biography,* perhaps for the purpose of delighting literary detectives such as myself. On page 273 of *Figures of Earth,* a character named Manuel asks rhetorically, "Is he the Horvendile whose great-toe is the morning star?" Cabell's novels are packed with such obscure odds and ends of mythological lore. *Jurgen,* for example, features some obscure figures from Russian folklore, such as the divinities of the seven days of the week (Pandelis, Sereda, and so on).

† He was not the only one to become fascinated with this idea. Goethe was so intrigued with the tale in Saxo Grammaticus that he came very close to composing a *Prince Amleth* of his own, which, had it been written, would have formed a curious contrast to the Shakespearian version.

So much for Eärendil—now what about Frodo? I
had, long before this stage of my investigation, decided
that Tolkien simply liked the name "Froda" in *Beowulf*, 28, and had borrowed it with no particular point
or purpose in mind. But while uncovering all this data
on the far-wandering star-hero and tracking him
through Tolkien and into Teutonic myth, I came
across a far more likely source in a portion of Saxo's
Gesta—the history of a king named "Frode." In the
second book of the *Gesta Danorum*, Frode, son of
Hadding, inherits a poor and penniless kingdom. A
certain traveler tells Frode that in a far island lies a
golden treasure guarded by a monstrous serpent—"a
snake wreathed in coils, doubled in many a fold, and
with tail drawn out in winding whorls, shaking his
manifold spirals and shedding venom," as Saxo puts it.
This mention of a serpent, or dragon, guarding treasure
brings to mind Tolkien's dragon-slaying scene in *The
Hobbit*. Sure enough, Saxo states that Frode kills the
serpent just as Bard the Archer kills Smaug (and
just as Siegfried slays Fafnir): "there is a place under
his lowest belly where thou mayst plunge the blade,"
says Saxo's character, and Frode kills the serpent
through an unprotected portion of his underside in the
grand tradition.

There are a couple of other anecdotes in Saxo
Grammaticus about this King Frode that make me
think the *Gesta Danorum* is the source from which
Tolkien borrowed the name. For instance, just as
Frodo wears a shirt of charmed mail, Frode also wore
a famous mail-coat that was magically rendered impervious to any weapon of pointed steel. And, rather sig-
nificantly, Frode is, like Frodo, associated with "gold

rings," for in the introduction to the Norroena Society edition of Saxo, Frederick Y. Powell remarks that this King Frode was so just and so feared across his realm that he "was able to hang up an arm-ring of gold in three parts of his kingdom that no thief for many years dared touch." And for the final touch, in Book Five of the *Gesta,* King Frode is for a time accompanied by a suspiciously Gandalf-like man of mystery, "the prophet Ygg, a man of unknown age, which was prolonged beyond the human span," as Saxo puts it.*

But, *mirabile dictu,* the most amazing is yet to come. In the saga of Halfdan the Black, I found Gandalf and Frode together as companions in an adventure. The saga tells of King Gandalf of Vingulmark, who wars against young Halfdan and who flees from the victorious young warrior-king. Later the sons of Gandalf, whose names are Hysing and Helsing, chal lenge Halfdan's dominion with a great army and force him into flight. He gathers his forces, returns, and conquers the sons of Gandalf at Eid, near Lake Oieren

The history of Halfdan is also told in the *Heims kringla* of Snorri Sturluson in substantially the same form. Snorri also gives the history of Harald Harfager, son of Halfdan, and tells how Harald is challenged by King Gandalf and his son Hake. An interesting pas-

---

* However, I was not wrong in my first assumption that "Frodo" was derived from the "Froda" mentioned in *Beowulf*. The passage in which the name Froda occurs reads:

> Betrothed is Freawaru, the young, the golden dame,
> To the glad son of Froda. For Hrothgar did devise ...

It refers to the marriage of the daughter of Hrothgar, the Danish lord at whose request Beowulf battles the ogre Grendel, to Ingeld, prince of the Heathobards, son of King Froda—the same person as Saxo's wise, just lawgiver, King Frode, as Frederick York Powell points out.

sage which puts Gandalf and Frode into direct proximity
appears in the first part of the *Heimskringla:* *

> After Halfdan the Black's death,
> many chiefs coveted the dominions
> he had left. Among these King Gandalf
> was the first; then Hogne and Frode,
> sons of Eystein, king of Hedemark.

Tolkien's mysterious divinities, the Valar or guard-
ians of the world, are an echo of the *vardir* of Norse
myth. This epithet is used regarding certain world-pro-
tecting deities mentioned by Rydberg in *Teutonic Mythology* (vol. 3, p. 754).

And the Elf queen Galadriel may owe something to
the traditional Gerda the Alf-Queen, who sounds much
like the Lady of Lothlorien: "In spite of the cloud that
hung over Asgard all was fair and peaceful in Alfheim.
Gerda, the radiant Alf-Queen, made there perpetual
sunshine with her bright face. The elves loved her, and
fluttered around her, keeping up a continual merry
chatter, which sounded through the land like the sharp
ripple of a brook over stony places; and Gerda answered
in low, sweet tones, as the answering wind sounds among
the trees." †

Shadowfax, the great steed belonging to the King of
the Mark, which Gandalf rides to Gondor, is another
example. The horse's name savors of Gullfaxi, or
Goldfax ("gold-mane"), the steed of the giant Hrung-
ner in Norse myth, as well as of Skinfaxi ("shining-

---

* For the story of Halfdan the Black and his wars against King
Gandalf, see *Heimskringla*, vol. 7 of the Noroenna series, pp. 6–9.
For the history of Harald Harfager, and the wars of Harald against
Gandalf, Frode, and others, see pp. 16–17.

† From A. and E. Keary, *The Heroes of Asgard.*

mane"), a steed mentioned in the third book of *The Elder Edda,* the *Vafthruthnismol,* 12, where it is said of him:

> the best of horses   to heroes he seems

I found other names in the *Edda* that Tolkien has used. Gimli, son of Glóin, is one of Frodo's companions on the Quest; "Gloin" is listed in the *Voluspo*'s dwarf catalogue, but not Gimli. He turns up as the name of a magical mountain, of all things, in stanza 64 of the *Voluspo.* The footnote to that verse defines the name "Gimli" as meaning "fire" or "gem." "Frea" (of the First Line of the Kings of the Mark, as given in the trilogy's Appendix A) obviously derives from the Norse goddess "Freya." "Gram," another King of the Mark, is a name borrowed from Sigurth's sword in *Regismol,* the twenty-first book of the *Edda.* And the notion of the curse-bearing Ring's seeming "heavy" to him who possesses it may come from the story of the enchanted necklace, Brisingamen, which Freya got from the Four Dwarves in the ninth book of the *Edda:*

> Brisingamen is dragging me down . . .
> Brisingamen is fair, but I find it heavy.

This necklace is under a curse and acts as the bane of its wearer, just like the One Ring in Tolkien. But the idea of magical rings with names and histories is very common in Norse legend; witness, for instance, the famous history of the ring Draupnir, forged by the dwarves Sindri and Brok, which can be found in almost any collection of Norse myths.

Remember the Orcs, the servants of Sauron? When I first began digging into the problem of Tolkien's sources, I presumed the name to be either pure invention, an anagram of the "Roc" from the *Arabian Nights,* or borrowed from the sea-monster called the Orc who appears in *Orlando Furioso.* But a lucky chance led me to a line in John Milton's Biblical epic, *Paradise Lost,* Bk. XI, lines 834–835:

> an island salt and bare,
> The haunt of seals and orcs, and sea-mew's clang

which started me off on an Orc hunt. I found out that in Milton orcs are (as in the French word, *orques*) some species of whale or grampus; this meaning is obviously what Ariosto had in mind, too, when he put one in the *Orlando.* But how did the Orc get into Tolkien?

I turned to *Beowulf,* 11, lines 111–114, and found:

> From him monsters   of all sorts were born:
> Etins and elves   and orcs, worst of all,
> Giant-folk also   who fought hard against God
> Long time agone.   God repaid them their sinning.

When I checked *Beowulf* in the original, I found the Anglo-Saxon form of the second line of that verse particularly interesting. It reads:

> *eotenas ond ylfe   ond orcnéas.*

Tolkien had therefore taken the word Orc from the Anglo-Saxon language—a promising discovery that led to much in the way of source-finding.* For example,

----

* Of course Tolkien does not mean to suggest his Orcs are *whales.* The word is used in that sense in *Beowulf,* but Tolkien doubtless

many of the names in and around the Mark of Rohan and Gondor and the Heirs of Anarion—names such as Eorl, Earnil, and Earnur—had at first seemed to me nothing more than echoes of *Beowulf*. That is, I had dismissed them as likely candidates for source hunting because I thought Tolkien had merely modeled these names on those of characters in the ancient Anglo-Saxon epic—names like "Eofor," "Eormenric," and so on. This did not prove to be the whole story, as my discovery of the origin of the Orcs indicated.

Consider, for a moment, King Théoden, Thengel's son, and his realm, the Mark. Now "Théoden" looks suspiciously like "Odin" and another name, "Denethor," looks like "Thor." But dig a little deeper. What does "the Mark" mean? The dictionary traces it back to the Old English *mearc* or "boundary" and defines it as "a tract of land held in common by a medieval community of freemen." In other words, it is not an invented name at all but an obsolete term for a division of land, just as Tolkien's Shire is an English word for a land division—a word still surviving in such place-names as Worcestershire and Lincolnshire.

With dictionary in hand, I realized that the Shire title "thain" was simply a variant on the old Scandinavian title "thane." And Tolkien's character "Eorl"— his name sounded to me like the Scandinavian title *jarl,* which became the English word "earl."

So far so good; but keeping in mind Tolkien's professional interest in old languages and his work in Anglo-Saxon, one can come closer to the whole

---

meant it in its alternate meaning. The Old English *orcnéas* comes from the Latin *orcus,* "hell; death." The meaning is actually "hell-corpses; monsters; evil spirits," and that sort of thing. The translator of the above-quoted passage of *Beowulf* seems to have erred in selecting the less likely of the two meanings for the word.

method. It is not just that "Théoden" sounds Norse or Anglo-Saxon—the very word *theoden* is Anglo-Saxon (spelled ðēoden); it means "chief of a tribe; ruler; prince; king." *

What about Théoden's father, Thengel? *Thengel* is also Anglo-Saxon: it is used in *Beowulf* to mean "prince." And Eorl does not just sound like the Danish original for "earl"—it, too, is Anglo-Saxon: *eorl* means "warrior; leader; chief; nobleman." Most of the other names in Rohan can be traced back to Anglo-Saxon meanings, given the patience to search for them and access to a good Old English dictionary.

I spent an amusing hour with Hall's *Concise* and found that "Grima Wormtongue" may have been inspired by *grimena* ("caterpillar"?); that the Hobbits' hillside houses, called smials and described as long narrow tunnels, probably came from the Anglo-Saxon word *smael,* defined as "thin; slender; narrow"; that the dark kingdom, Mordor, was derived from the Anglo-Saxon *morthor* (morðor), "murder", in *Beowulf;* with the additional meanings of "punishment; torment; misery."

As for the Ents, Tolkien's giant tree shepherds? *Ent* is the Anglo-Saxon word for "giant." The Hobbit word "mathom," which may be defined as something one does not really want but hates to throw away, relates to the Anglo-Saxon word *maðem,* which means "treasure; jewel; ornament; gift." The name of the ferocious wolves of the wild—the Warg—in *The Hobbit* was borrowed by Tolkien from the Anglo-Saxon *wearg—*

---

* For this research, I used J. R. Clark Hall's *A Concise Anglo-Saxon Dictionary*, fourth edition, Cambridge, 1960. I am indebted to a Tolkien fan, Barry Greene, for calling this source to my attention.

"wolf; accursed or wicked one"—which is probably cognate with the Old Icelandic word *vargr,* used for "wolf" and "outlaw."

An exploration of the Anglo-Saxon language will reveal many ways in which the Professor used it for the names of characters, perhaps for place names, and for words in some of his Middle-earth languages.* I will let these few samples serve to prove my point, rather than try to compile a complete list of all his usages. Any reader who likes may find many more than the few I have given above.

---

* The Welsh language is another fruitful source. Very many of Tolkien's place names seem to be modeled on Welsh names, and I am told by members of The Tolkien Society of America that his Elvish language has many direct resemblances to Welsh.

16.
Some People, Places, and Things

It is not down on any map; true places never are.
HERMAN MELVILLE, *Moby Dick*

~~~~~~

PLACES

Tolkien's geography bears little or no resemblance
to the world we live in, although in theory at least the
reader is supposed to think of it as our own world at
some prehistoric epoch. But this device is more of a
convenience than a meaningful insight; that is, were
the world of the Ring presented as some other planet,
Tolkien would be forced to create a complete zoology
and botany of extraterrestrial lifeforms, as Edgar Rice
Burroughs did in his novels laid on "Barsoom"
(Mars). Rather, Tolkien used the simple device of setting the stage of his story in mythological times. Both
of these alternate techniques have been exploited by
the various writers of heroic fantasy discussed in previous chapters. E. R. Eddison, who laid the scene of
The Worm Ouroboros on Mercury, was forced into all
manner of untenable plot artifices to account for this,
and his novel is riddled with internal self-contradic-
tions (such as Mercurian characters quoting from
Sappho, Herrick, Donne, Webster, and Shakespeare).
Tolkien's solution to this dilemma is a favorite one

184

with many fantasy writers. The adventure fantasies of Robert E. Howard (which are of a subgenre called Sword and Sorcery * and not, strictly speaking, epic fantasy in the Morris-Dunsany-Eddison-Tolkien tradition at all) are also laid in an era before history proper, a few thousand years after the submergence of Atlantis and some millennia prior to the rise of Egypt and Ur of the Chaldees.

But while Tolkien's maps of Middle-earth are roughly cognate with northeastern Europe, it is impossible to correlate them with any historical accuracy with early maps of Europe. They still provide a certain scholarly interest, however.

According to the Tolkien version of prehistory, the earliest events in Middle-earth would seem to be the very ancient division of the Elves into two major races. The Elves, the *Quendi,* split into two groupings: the first of these is the Three Kindreds of the *Eldar,* who began westward to find the Undying Realm in the Uttermost West; the second, whose name I cannot find in Tolkien, is the East Elves and does not play any part in the story of the trilogy. This division of the Elves occurred at some remote era called "the Elder Days,"

---

* The phrase was coined to describe simple, direct, pulp action stories which pit brawny barbarian heroes, armed with broadswords and the like, against evil magicians or supernatural monsters. The subgenre was more or less created by Robert E. Howard (1906–1936) with his "Conan of Cimmeria" stories, written for the magazine *Weird Tales.* Many later writers have imitated or continued in Howard's vein, such as L. Sprague de Camp with his novel *The Tritonian Ring* (1953), the late Henry Kuttner with his "Elak of Atlantis" stories, and myself, for that matter, with my six-novel series about "Thongor of Lemuria." The term Sword and Sorcery was invented to delineate this subspecies of heroic fantasy about 1961, by Fritz Leiber, who is himself probably the greatest living master of this sort of fictional swashbuckling. The derivation by analogue with "blood and thunder" and "cloak and dagger" is obvious.

and it would seem to indicate that the original home of the Elvish race is somewhere in the far east beyond Mordor, but this interpretation seems unlikely, and I may be making an error of interpretation.

The *Eldar,* the West-Elves, are made up of three Kindreds, the *Noldor,* the *Sindar* (or Grey Elves), and a third tribe which Tolkien does not seem to have named. They ventured across Middle-earth and took to the sea. Sailing west from the coast, they came first to Númenor, "the westernmost of all mortal lands," then to the Isle of Eressëa, and finally to the Undying Realm itself, which seems to be called Valinor. And there the Elves remained until they were forced by the rise of evil forces on Middle-earth to form the Host of Valinor and return to Middle-earth to save the world. In that war they broke Thangorodrim and overwhelmed Morgoth, and the First Age ended. Most of the Noldor and the Sindar returned into the Uttermost West, but a certain portion remained behind in the mortal lands. These are the Elves that we encounter during the action of the trilogy, and with the end of *The Lord of the Rings* the last of them are returning to Valinor; in the conclusion of the story, Gandalf, Bilbo, and Frodo depart with them from the Havens.

Much of this story bears a certain resemblance to portions of the history of the faerie race as given in the ancient Irish mythological literature. These faeries are not leprechauns or pookas, but the heroic, kingly, and godlike race of superhumanly beautiful and wise beings the old Irish mythographers called the Tuatha de Danaan. Their history is given in more or less fragmented form in a number of very ancient Celtic manuscripts, of which the earliest known is the *Würzburg Codex,* which dates from about A.D. 700. Some of these collec-

tions of old manuscripts have names which remind one
of Tolkien's "the Red Book of Westmarch" (the supposed source from which the trilogy was written)—
like the *Leabhar Buidhe Lecain* (the Yellow Book of
Lecan) or the *Leabhar Mór Lecain* (the Great Book
of Lecan), both of which date from the late four-
teenth or early fifteenth century.

The history of the Tuatha de Danaan (the Children
of the Goddess Dan) is given in the *Leabhar Gabhála*
(the Book of Invasions), but it is not all in one piece
but is scattered among several other books, such as the
Leabhar Laighneach (the Book of Leinster) and
Leabhar Baile an Mhota (the Book of Ballymote).
The text of the Book of Invasions was pieced together
with the help of others by Irish scholar Michael
O'Clery about the year 1630.

Briefly, the story is this. The Tuatha were driven
into exile from their heavenly Otherworld and came to
Earth in the days when a race called the Firbolg ruled
Ireland. They came from the four cities of Falias, Gor-
ias, Finias, and Murias, and brought with them four
magical treasures, the Lia Fail (a stone), the Sword of
Lug, his Spear, and the Cauldron of the Gods. According to a tradition quoted in *The White Goddess* by
Robert Graves, they arrived in the British Isles in the
year 1472 B.C.* At the famous Battle of Moytura, the
Tuatha conquered the Firbolg and ruled in their place.
Later, during an invasion by another people, the Mile-
sians (in 1268 B.C., says Mr. Graves), the Tuatha

---

* Mr. Graves' book, a fantastic compendium of oddities of classical
lore and exotic information, is packed with other similar rare
"facts." He gives the date of the victory of Zeus over the Titans as
1515 B.C.; the voyage of the *Argo* expedition as 1225 B.C.; and the
Fall of Troy as 1183 B.C.

were themselves overcome at the Battle of Tailtenn and lost their divine status, dwindling into mere tutelary spirits of mound, hill, and wood—the *sidhe* (pronounced "shee") of Irish legend. Eventually they left the world of men altogether and ventured back into the Tir na nOg—the Celtic paradise—from which, ages before, they had come.

This looks quite a bit like the history of the Eldar as given in Tolkien. The Tuatha seem to have entered this world somewhere around the Greek isles, from which they traveled westward until reaching the coast of Europe, voyaging across the sea to the British Isles from there. This is just about what Tolkien's Elves seem to have done; Númenor and Erresëa may then correspond to Britain and Ireland, if we accept the Tuatha as being Tolkien's Elves.*

But there is a better clue to Tolkien's reference in Númenor. He explains that under their last king, Ar-Pharazôn the Golden, the Númenoreans were tempted by Sauron and sought to land in the Forbidden Realm of Valinor in defiance of the Ban long imposed upon them by the Valar. Then: "when Ar-Pharazôn set foot upon the shores of Aman the Blessed, the Valar laid

---

* Historians now feel that there may be a certain amount of historical fact in this old Celtic myth of the migration of the Tuatha de Danaan. There are otherwise unexplainable references to a mysterious *Danuna* people engraved on the Karatepe bilingual, and a tribe called the *Dananian* is listed, among others, in temple inscriptions dating from the reign of Rameses III. Homer also makes mention of a cryptic people called the *Danaoi*. If all of this makes sense, then Mr. Graves' date of 1472 B.C. for their arrival in Britain may not be too far off the mark. See Leonard Cottrell's book *Lost Cities* for a discussion of the mysterious "people of the sea" who were migrating across Europe somewhere around the late thirteenth century B.C. They were defeated by the Egyptians about that time in a series of land and sea battles, and the Egyptian victory is commemorated in the Rameses III temple inscription.

down their Guardianship and called upon the One, and the world was changed. Númenor was thrown down and swallowed in the Sea." *

In other words: Númenor is Atlantis, the Lost Continent, which Plato located somewhere in mid-Atlantic, off the shores of southern Spain.

Valinor itself is not quite part of this world at all, but separate from it, very much as the Celtic Tir na nOg is "apart" from the other lands. "And the Undying Lands were removed forever from the circles of the world," says the Appendix. Valinor, the home of the Elves, is equated with Tir na nOg.

The conclusion is inescapable: Valinor is Fairyland.

A final note on the places. The realm of Gondor might derive from "Gondul," a Valkyrie mentioned in the thirty-first stanza of the *Voluspo*. But a much better guess would be that Tolkien dug the name out of an atlas (a trick many fantasy writers use); for Gondor is a province of Ethiopia.

PEOPLE

In my earlier chapters tracing the evolution of the epic fantasy novel little mention was made of the archetypes of the characters in the fantasy epic and the point in the evolution of the genre at which they became established. Let us take a brief look at Tolkien's protagonists.

Of course Aragorn is the perfect Patrician Hero. As with King Arthur, his background and parentage are obscure and dim but later revealed as royal. Like

---

* *LOTR,* Appendix A, I, p. 392.

Amadis of Gaul, he is known under various names at various points in the story.* And like Siegfried, he bears a charmed sword that was once broken and has now been reforged and given a new name.

Frodo, however, is a different kind of hero. He is not born of kingly parentage and obviously destined for high, heroic deeds "far on the ringing plains of windy Troy." In Shakespeare's phrase, Frodo is one of those who "have greatness thrust upon them"—the ordinary person who rises to heroic stature through the course of events. Since we, too, are nonheroic, ordinary folk, we easily identify with him. Frodo is also, however, the tragic and suffering figure, who bears without complaint a burden too terrible for others to bear. In this he is Christlike. But Tolkien is too subtle a writer to deal in easy archetypes. Frodo learns, slowly and painfully, how to become a hero. Nor is he perfect and pure: in fact, he is guilty of three foolish mistakes and is punished for each by a wound from which he is never to completely recover. His first error is folly, and his punishment is the knife wound he suffers on Weathertop; his second, overconfidence, for which his punishment is to taste the sting of Shelob; his third is weakness itself when, at the brink of the Crack of Doom, he does not prove strong enough to hurl the Ring away. His punishment for that greatest of his three sins is the most gruesome of all—the loss of his ring finger when Gollum bites it off to get the Ring from him.† Aragorn, then, is the very pattern

---

* Tolkien's character is variously called the Dúnadan, Strider, Aragorn, Elessar, and Elfstone. At different points in his history, Amadis is known as Child of the Sea, Beltenebros, the Green Knight, the Greek Knight, and so forth.

† For many of these points I am indebted to science-fantasy writer and Tolkien-enthusiast, Marion Zimmer Bradley, and her long and

and prototype of the Quest Hero; Frodo is the ordinary man, forced by painful circumstances to find within himself the sources of courage and strength.

Miss Bradley points out: "It is traditional in Quest literature that the hero should have a comic-relief satellite; but Sam, though occasionally witty, is not really a figure of comedy; not in the sense that Papageno, in *The Magic Flute,* is a comic figure." The comic element is not so much in Sam as it is in Sam's contrast to his surroundings. For he is a plain, blunt, honest, loyal, wise, but unlettered son of the soil, and what humor lurks about him is more a matter of incongruity than of true humor. His plain, sensible, straight-forward manner of speaking forms amusing contrast to the heroic events through which he passes and the gallant, high-born, princely personages with whom he comes into contact. It is also amusing when simple, common, practical Sam becomes—as here and there he does become—a bold, heroic, valorous figure in his own right. It would be a considerable error to regard Sam as merely the Sancho Panza of the piece, for Sancho is in himself, in his words and attitudes and deeds, very much the clown, although he is also capable of common sense and practicality, in contrast to the foggy-minded chivalrous nonsense of the ingenious gentleman of La Mancha.

Gandalf, on the other hand, seems very much the archetypal figure—the Wise Old Man, the Friendly Magician (to use the Jungian symbols). A cursory look at him makes him seem one with other literary magicians—Dr. Vandermast in E. R. Eddison's Zimiamvian Trilogy, or Dr. Meliboë in Fletcher Pratt's

well-thought-out essay on the trilogy, "Men, Halflings and Hero Worship." First published in 1961, it was later reprinted in *Niekas,* No. 16, June 30, 1966.

marvelous novel *The Well of the Unicorn,* or even wise old Merlyn in T. H. White's Arthurian prose epic *The Once and Future King* and Cabell's Miramon Llaguor in *Figures of Earth.* But he is very much more than just the Enchanter, the hero's wise companion who can work a bit of the old hocus-pocus to get the hero out of a quandary. In a very deep and real sense of the word, Gandalf is the actual hero of the book, the truly central character. Throughout the entire tale, Gandalf—and Gandalf alone—is in complete possession of all relevant information at every point. Gandalf already knows everything the other characters have to slowly learn. Gandalf knows about Treebeard and the Ents and Tom Bombadil and the true importance of the Ring, and it is usually Gandalf who explains about them to the other characters. Like Aragorn, Gandalf is also a high-born and noble being of mysterious lineage. Like Frodo, he is a real person—honest, cantankerous, filled with humor and joy. And like Frodo, Gandalf suffers in a Christlike way. For during the course of the story Gandalf is slain and passes through death to a greater region of life beyond, returning to the lands of men with powers greater than before, purged of human frailties and errors.

At first—given the birthday party and tinkering with fireworks and dropping in for tea with Bilbo—Gandalf seems a small, frail, little old man, fussy, vain, and faintly comical. The problem is, then, to reconcile this creature with the real Gandalf, whom we glimpse only briefly in the trilogy, in those moments of ultimate peril and ultimate need when he reveals himself as a towering, shining figure of tremendous power and authority. At such times—as when Gandalf confronts the terrible Balrog on the bridge leading out of the Mines of Moria—he not only seems more than just a mere magician, he seems more than just a mortal man. We have a glimpse of the god apparently concealed behind his white or gray robes.

Let us look further at Tolkien's information about Gandalf. The chronology in Appendix A reveals that at the period of Bilbo's birthday party he has already been alive on Middle-earth for something like two thousand years. And this is only part of his history, for the Appendix adds:

> The *Istari* or Wizards appeared in Middle-earth. It was afterwards said that they came out of the Far West [i.e. Valinor or Faerie] and were messengers sent to contest the power of Sauron. . . . They came therefore in the shape of Men, though they were never young and aged only slowly, and they had many powers of mind and hand. *They revealed their true name to few.* [Appendix B, p. 455]

The italics are mine. Since Tolkien said "their true name" instead of "their true names," he must have something other than a personal name in mind. He seems to mean: they revealed *what they really were* only to a few.*

If Gandalf came into Middle-earth out of Valinor, as this quotation seems to indicate, then he may perhaps be one of the Lords of Faerie—in other words, an Elf disguised as a Man. But Gandalf is not in any way Elflike. Tolkien characterizes and describes the Elves and their ways in very precise terms: Gandalf is simply not at all like an Elf. What, then, could he be?

---

* I may be wrong on this. In the Ballantine edition, revised by Tolkien, the text of this passage reads "their true name*s*." This may be a deliberate revision, or a typographical error, or the correction of a typographical error in the original hard-cover edition. No one seems to know, but I mention it just for the sake of completeness.

Besides the High Elves, the Valar dwell in or around Valinor. Thus Gandalf may be one of the gods who are charged by the One with the guardianship of the world. He is known by many different names; to the Elves he is "Mithrandir" the Grey Pilgrim; to the inhabitants of the Shire he is "Gandalf the Grey"; the Rohirrim refer to him as "Stormcrow," "Greyhame," and "The White Rider."

The Norse myths tell of a figure very like Gandalf, who, when he moves among men, also goes disguised as an old wanderer with a gray beard and a tattered cloak, leaning upon a staff. He, too, is known by many different names: in *The Elder Edda,* he is variously called the Old One, the Wanderer, Ygg, Herjan the Leader of Hosts, Sigfather, Hropt, Tveggi, Hor the High One, and so on. He is the God Odin.

The word "Gandalf" in the *Edda* means "magic-elf," which would certainly be appropriate if Gandalf came from Valinor. The Odin of the Norse also passes as a magician among men, according to this verse from the *Baldrs Draumar,* stanza 2, in the *Edda*: "Then Othin rose, the enchanter old." And in the following stanza he is also called "the father of magic." Elsewhere in the *Edda* Odin is referred to as the God of Magic.

I suspect that Gandalf the Grey Wizard—who came into Middle-earth thousands of years before from the Uttermost West, who goes disguised as a man but is not a man, who is known by different names in different lands, who is capable of passing through death and emerging greater than before—is Tolkien's version of Odin, the Father of the Gods, Lord of Asgard, and is actually one of the Valar. Perhaps we may learn something of his true nature in *The Silmarillion* when it eventually reaches print.

A few last words about names. One of the most interesting and original characters in all the trilogy is the merry, singing, ageless little nature-sprite, Tom Bombadil. His name is strikingly similar to *Boabdil*, a popular figure in Islamic legend. There are many references to Boabdil in Washington Irving's curious collection of travel notes and Moorish legend, *The Alhambra* (1832). Boabdil (his actual name was Abu-Abdallah) was the last of the Moorish kings of Granada, who gave up his realm to Ferdinand of Castile, looked his last upon the magnificent city where he had reigned, and crossed over into Africa, never to return. He became a melancholy, haunting figure in Moorish romantic legend thereafter.

THINGS

In the first volume of the trilogy, when the White Council convenes at the House of Elrond, the Half-elven prince recounts the legend of the White Tree which once bloomed in Minas Arnor in the great days of Gondor. "There in the courts of the King grew a white tree, from the seed of that tree which Isildur brought over the deep waters, and the seed of that tree before came from Eressëa, and before that out of the Uttermost West in the Day before days when the world was young." The Tree of Gondor is long since dead. But at the end of the trilogy, as Aragorn claims his kingdom, Gandalf takes him to the height of a mountain and shows Aragorn his kingdom laid out beneath him. Aragorn cries out: "The Tree in the Court of the Fountain is still withered and barren. When shall I see a sign that it will ever be otherwise?" Gandalf then shows him a sapling tree sprouting at the edge of the snow, high up on the mountainous heights above Gondor. It is indeed a sapling of the White Tree itself, that ancient and mysterious symbol of kingship, fertility, and power—a talismanic link between Gondor and the West.

In volume III of *Teutonic Mythology*, Viktor Rydberg describes a tradition very similar to Gondor's White Tree. He writes: "Popular traditions scattered over Sweden, Denmark, and Germany have to this day been preserved, on the lips of the common people. . . . Common to most of these traditions, both the Northern and the German, is the feature that . . . when the greatest distress is at hand, or when the end of the world approaches and the day of judgement comes . . . when the trumpets of the last day sound, a great battle with the powers of evil (Antichrist) is to be fought, *an immensely old tree, which has withered, is to grow green again, and a happier age is to begin*" [italics added].

In Appendix A to the trilogy, Tolkien gives a summary of events in the First Age of Middle-earth. He tells of Beren and Lúthien, how "Together they wrested a *silmaril* from the Iron Crown of Morgoth." There are other references to this Iron Crown in the trilogy, and doubtless we shall hear much about it in *The Silmarillion*.

Tolkien may very well have read of the famous Iron Crown of the Roman Emperor Constantine, which his mother, St. Helena, fashioned for him. Although unadorned with magic gems such as the *silmaril*, the Iron Crown of Constantine was not without certain rare associations, for St. Helena imbedded in its circlet one of the Sacred Nails used in the Crucifixion. The Iron Crown survived the collapse of the Empire of the West. It was given by Pope Gregory the First to Theodolinde for her zeal in converting the Lombards to the Faith, and it became known in the Middle Ages as the Iron Crown of Lombardy. This same crown was used in the coronations of Charlemagne, Sigismund, Charles V, and the Emperor Napoleon. I believe it is still preserved, one of the rarest and most unusual treasures surviving from antiquity, with its incredible wealth of historical associations.

Postscript: After Tolkien

~~~~~~

If L. Sprague de Camp is correct in his opinion that Lord Dunsany was the most influential fantasy writer of the first half of this century, then I feel certain that J. R. R. Tolkien will prove the greatest influence over writers in the last half. The first signs of this influence are already visible.

In England and America a number of new writers are beginning to produce books that show Tolkien's influence. About the earliest of these was Carol Kendall, who published a children's fantasy novel called *The Gammage Cup* in 1959. It seems considerably influenced by *The Hobbit.* * Miss Kendall tells of a Hob

---

* I have often wondered if *The Hobbit* itself does not show certain traces of having been influenced by a strange and lovely fantasy novel for children, *The Three Mulla-Mulgars* by poet Walter de la Mare. It was first published in 1910, when Tolkien was eighteen years old. De la Mare's three heroes—curious, quaint little creatures—dwell in the Forest of Munza; therein the folk worship or fear strange deities such as Nōōmanossi, and Immanâla the Queen of Shadows. The author tells of unknown beasts, the Mamasul, the Impaleena; of Dragon-trees, Samarak-creepers, Ollaconda; of Earth-mulgars, "groping, gluttonous, cannibal gnomes," and other unfamiliar creatures. The three heroes are descended from Assasimmon, the Prince of the Valleys of Tishnar. They embark on a perilous and magical quest into his distant realm, bearing with them a fantastic and rare treasure, the glowing, milk-white Wonderstone of Tishnar. Many dangers befall them; while crossing the seven peaks of the Mountains of Arakkaboa, they are attacked by fierce eagles; one of the characters is taken prisoner by a monstrous, barbaric Oomgar who enslaves him for a time; they encounter the great shaggy Mountain-mulgars and are pursued by snow-wolves. At last,

bitlike race of little people dwelling in quaint houses in a rural valley surrounded and protected by high mountains. In these mountains dwell their ancient foes—repulsive, goblinish beings, from whom the little folk escaped to find refuge in the valley. An expedition of the Five Heroes goes into these mountains, for the goblinlike foes are stirring anew. The heroes are armed with charmed swords which glow with fierce light when the foe is near—all very like Tolkien. In a sequel, *The Whisper of Glocken* (1965), Miss Kendall describes the quest for an ancient treasure which throws her heroes in conflict with a huge, brutal, Orclike race called the Hulks.

A book by Alan Garner, *The Weirdstone of Brisingamen* (1960), seems more influenced by *LOTR*. Drawing from Pictish and Nordic-British legendary materials, Garner tells an exciting, heroic tale of the epic struggle between Cadellin, the wise old enchanter, and Nastrond, the Great Spirit of Darkness. In a sequel, *The Moon of Gomrath* (1963), Garner utilizes Welsh, Gaelic, and Highlands Scots lore for his background mythos. These two novels are filled with invented beings—monsters, noble and gallant warrior-elves, and the like—and they have won a faithful readership. A third novel by the same author, *Elidor* (1965), is unrelated to the earlier books but is still a fantasy involved with travel between magic half-worlds and our own planet.

Probably the finest of recent novels which seem to

---

on the very borders of Tishnar, a weird lake-dwelling woman creature called a Water-Midden wheedles and tricks the Wonderstone from its bearer. The resemblances between this book and *The Hobbit* are not so much a matter of plot or background myth, as in the very style and substance of Mr. de la Mare's prose, singing, magical, studded with phrases and words in his invented languages, filled with verses and songs.

show the influence of Professor Tolkien are the Prydain books by the American writer Lloyd Alexander. His five brilliant and well-written fantasy novels about the Welsh otherworld of Prydain began with *The Book of Three* (1964), which introduced his hero, Taran, in boyhood, apprenticed to a powerful, benign old magician.* In the sequel, *The Black Cauldron* (1965), and in *The Castle of Llyr* (1966) we watch Taran growing into young manhood. The two concluding volumes of the series, *Taran Wanderer* (1967) and *The High King* (1968), show him in his manhood.

Alexander has gone very deeply into Welsh mythological lore, a field largely untouched even by scholars. His prime source of course is the great central text of the Welsh mythology, *The Mabinogion,* one of the world's great books. Mr. Alexander's characters adventure across this imagined early medieval world, encountering evil magicians, monsters, brutal outlaws and bandits, enchantresses and hags. They quest for magical treasures, venture into faerie realms, and deal with dwarves and other curious beings, including a startlingly original giant. It is a measure of Alexander's skill as a writer that his books emerge as something more than just "Tolkienian." He has absorbed and digested his influences and created books stamped with his own imaginative gifts in every line. The Prydain books have won a very enthusiastic and sizable following, which they richly deserve.

To my knowledge there have not as yet appeared any fully adult works of epic fantasy which show the

---

* Lloyd Alexander has told me he is about equally influenced by Tolkien and T. H. White. *The Book of Three* has obvious resemblances to *The Sword in the Stone*. In that book, the young boy, Wart, is under the tutelage of Merlyn the Magician.

marks of Tolkien's influence. But I know at least two writers who are working in the genre. And I have myself for some ten years, off and on, been puttering with an epic fantasy of enormous length in the Morris-Dunsany-Eddison-Tolkien tradition. When and if it is completed and published, it will be called *Khymyrium: The City of the Hundred Kings, from the Coming of Aviathar the Lion to the Passing of Spheridion the Doomed.*

Appendix A

A Checklist of Critical Literature on The Lord of the Rings

The following is by no means intended to represent a complete, exhaustive listing of every article on Tolkien that has been published in magazines or newspapers to date. Except for three or four rather important specimens, I have ignored most straight book reviews. And I have deliberately neglected to include in this Checklist the popular articles written for the general public in mass-circulation magazines—again, with a couple of exceptions. I have, for my own convenience, arranged the listing alphabetically by author in roughly chronological sequence. I am indebted to Alexis Levitin of The Tolkien Society of America for some of the following information.

1955. Lewis, C. S. "Dethronement of Power," *Time and Tide*, October.
1956. Auden, W. H. "At The End of the Quest, Victory," *The New York Times Book Review*, January 22.
    Halle, Louis J. "History Through the Mind's Eye," *The Saturday Review*, January.
    Parker, Douglas. "Hwaet We Holbytla," *The Hudson Review,* Winter 1956–57.
    Straight, Michael. "The Fantastic World of Professor Tolkien," *The New Republic,* January.
    Wilson, Edmund. "Oo, Those Awful Orcs!" *The Nation,* April 14.
1959. Blissett, William. "The Despots of The Rings," *The South Atlantic Quarterly,* Summer.
    Spacks, Patricia. "Ethical Patterns in *The Lord of the Rings,*" *Critique,* Spring-Fall.
1961. Bradley, Marion Zimmer. "Men, Halflings and Hero Wor-

ship," privately published pamphlet, 1961; reprinted in *Niekas,* No. 16, June 30, 1966.

Carter, Lin. "Notes on Tolkien, Part I: Theme and Form," *Xero,* No. 7, November.

Irwin, W. R. "There and Back Again," *Sewanee Review,* Fall.

1962. Carter, Lin. "Notes on Tolkien, Part II: Names and Places," *Xero,* No. 8, May.

"Notes on Tolkien, Part III: Sources and Influences," *Xero,* No. 9, September.

1963. Reilly, R. J. "Tolkien and the Fairy Story," *Thought,* Spring.

1966. Beagle, Peter S. "Tolkien's Magic Ring," *Holiday,* June; reprinted as preface to *The Tolkien Reader,* New York, Ballantine Books.

Carter, Lin. "What About This Tolkien Fellow, Anyway?" *Triumph,* November.

Resnik, Henry. "The Hobbit-Forming World of J. R. R. Tolkien," *The Saturday Evening Post,* July 2.

1968. Ready, W. *The Tolkien Relation, a Personal Inquiry,* Chicago, Henry Regnery Company; reprinted in paperback as *Understanding Tolkien,* New York, Paperback Library, Inc., January 1969.

Appendix B

A Selected Bibliography

More than 250 books were read or consulted during the writing of this book or are mentioned therein. Were I to list every single title, the length of this bibliography would be out of all proportion to its value. I have therefore limited myself to listing only those books directly quoted from or discussed prominently in my text—those books which a reader might reasonably expect more information on than is given in the text itself. I have not bothered to list the various titles by Professor Tolkien here, assuming that sufficient information on each of them appears in the text. Nor have I felt it necessary to give space in this bibliography to standard works such as Homer, Shakespeare, the Bible, or *Alice*. Listings are arranged alphabetically by author, and where more than one title by a single author is given, as in a series, I have chosen to list them in chronological sequence of publication, for clarity. Works of unknown authorship are listed at the beginning, under ANON., alphabetically by title.

ANON.: *Beowulf,* translated by William Ellery Leonard, New York, The Heritage Press, 1939.

The Epic of Gilgamesh, translated and with an introduction by N. K. Sandars, Baltimore, The Penguin Classics, 1960.

Hesiod, The Homeric Hymns, and Homerica, translated by Hugh G. Evedyn-White, London, William Heinemann, Ltd., 1959. For information on the Cyclic poets discussed in Chapter 10, see the introduction, pp. ix–xlviii, and the section on the Epic Cycle, pp. 481–539.

The Nibelungenlied, translated from the German by Margaret Armour, with an introduction by Franz Schoenberner, New York, The Heritage Press, 1961.

The Poem of the Cid, translated by Lesley Byrd Simpson, Berkeley, University of California Press, 1957.

The Poetic Edda, translated, with an introduction and notes, by Henry Adams Bellows, New York, The American-Scandinavian Foundation, 1957. This is the edition of *The Elder Edda* used throughout this book.

Richard the Lion-Hearted (and Other Medieval English Romances), translated and edited by Bradford B. Broughton, New York, E. P. Dutton and Co., Inc., 1966. For the verse quoted at the head of Chapter 12, see p. 149.

The Saga of King Heidrek the Wise, translated from the Icelandic and edited, with introduction, notes, and appendices, by Christopher Tolkien, London, Thomas Nelson and Sons, Ltd., 1960. One of a series issued under the title of Nelson's Icelandic Texts.

The Song of Roland, translated by Charles Scott Moncrieff, with an introduction by Hamish Miles, New York, The Heritage Press, n.d.

The Song of William, translated by Edward Noble Stone, Seattle, University of Washington Press, 1951. The verse quoted in a footnote to Chapter 11 may be found on p. 60.

Volsunga Saga, translated by William Morris, with an introduction by Robert W. Gutman, New York, Collier Books, 1962.

Alexander, Lloyd. *The Book of Three,* New York, Holt, Rinehart and Winston, 1964.

———. *The Black Cauldron,* New York, Holt, Rinehart and Winston, 1965.

———. *The Castle of Llyr,* New York, Holt, Rinehart and Winston, 1966.

———. *Taran Wanderer,* New York, Holt, Rinehart and Winston, 1967.

———. *The High King,* New York, Holt, Rinehart and Winston, 1968.

Anderson, Poul. *The Broken Sword,* New York, Abelard-Schuman, Inc., 1954.

Apollonius (of Rhodes). *The Argonautica,* translated by Edward P. Coleridge, New York, The Heritage Press, 1960.

Bowra, Maurice. *Heroic Poetry,* London, 1952. A source used in Chapters 10, 11, and 12.

Cabell, James Branch. *Figures of Earth (A Comedy of Appearances),* New York, Robert M. McBride and Co., 1925.

————. *The Cream of the Jest (A Comedy of Evasions)*, New York, Robert M. McBride and Co., 1927.

————. *The Silver Stallion (A Comedy of Redemption)*, London, John Lane, The Bodley Head, Ltd., 1928.

————. *Jurgen (A Comedy of Justice)*, New York, Robert M. McBride and Co., 1929.

————. *Something About Eve (A Comedy of Fig-leaves)*, New York, Robert M. McBride and Co., 1929.

————. (as "Branch Cabell"). *Hamlet Had an Uncle (A Comedy of Honor)*, New York, Farrar and Rinehart, Inc., 1940.

Cervantes Saavedra, Miguel de. *Don Quixote (The Ingenious Gentleman of La Mancha)*, translated from the Spanish by John Ormsby, with an introduction by Irwin Edman, New York, The Heritage Press, n. d. For Cervantes' judgment of *Amadis*, quoted in Chapter 12, see pp. 72–75; for information on other romances mentioned in Chapter 12, see the Notes to this chapter, pp. 75–78.

Cottrell, Leonard. *Lost Cities*, New York, Universal Library, 1963. For information on the possible historicity of the Tuatha de Danaan and their migration through the Near East, as given in Chapter 16, see pp. 104–108.

De Camp, L. Sprague. *The Tritonian Ring (and Other Pusadian Tales)*, New York, Twayne Publishers, 1953. A heroic fantasy novel strictly in the Howard tradition, but of interest to Tolkien readers.

De la Mare, Walter. *The Three Mulla-Mulgars*, New York, Alfred A. Knopf, 1919.

De Moraes, Francisco. *Palmerin of England*, an anonymous English translation, London, Longman, Hurst, Rees, and Orme, 1807. A splendid example of the better imitations of *Amadis*.

Dippold, George Theodore. *The Great Epics of Medieval Germany*, Boston, Little, Brown and Co., 1882. A source used in Chapters 11, 12, 14, and 16.

Dunsany, Lord. *The Gods of Pegāna*, London, Elkin Mathews, 1905.

————. *The Book of Wonder (A Chronicle of Little Adventures at the Edge of the World)*, London, Elkin Mathews, 1912. Contains stories discussed or quoted from in Chapter 13, such as "The Bridge of the Man-Horse," "Thangobrind the Jeweller," "The City of Never," and "The Hoard of the Gibbelins."

————. *A Dreamer's Tales (and Other Stories)*, with an introduction by Padraic Colum, New York, The Modern Library, n. d. Contains "Carcassonne," "The Sword of Welleran," and "The Fortress Unvanquishable," discussed in Chapter 13.

―――. *The King of Elfland's Daughter,* London, G. P. Putnam's Sons, 1924. Dunsany's most interesting heroic fantasy novel, of great interest to Tolkien fans.

Eddison, E. R. *Styrbiorn the Strong,* New York, Albert and Charles Boni, 1926.

―――. *The Worm Ouroboros,* New York, E. P. Dutton and Co., Inc., 1952.

―――. *Mistress of Mistresses,* New York, E. P. Dutton and Co., Inc., 1935.

―――. *A Fish Dinner at Memison,* New York, E. P. Dutton and Co., Inc., 1941.

―――. *The Mezentian Gate,* edited and privately printed by Colin R. Eddison, 1958.

Ferdowsi (sic). *The Epic of the Kings (Shah-nama, the National Epic of Persia),* translated by Reuben Levy, Chicago, The University of Chicago Press, 1966. The histories of Zal and Rustum alluded to in Chapter 12 may be found in Books V, VI, IX, XI, XIV.

Garner, Alan. *The Weirdstone of Brisingamen,* New York, Ace Books, Inc., 1966. Originally published by Franklin Watts, 1961.

―――. *The Moon of Gomrath,* London, Collins, 1963.

―――. *Elidor,* London, Collins, 1965.

Graves, Robert. *The White Goddess (A Historical Grammar of Poetic Myth),* New York, Creative Age Press, 1948.

Haight, Elizabeth Hazelton. *More Essays on Greek Romances,* New York, Longmans, Green and Co., 1945. A source of information on early romances in general and the fabulous history of Alexander the Great in particular.

Hall, J. R. Clark. *A Concise Anglo-Saxon Dictionary,* fourth edition, Cambridge University Press, 1960.

Holmes, Urban Tigner, Jr. *History of Old French Literature,* University of North Carolina Press, 1948. For background information on the history of the *chanson de geste* discussed in Chapter 11.

Howard, Robert E. *Conan the Conqueror,* edited and with an introduction by L. Sprague de Camp, New York, Lancer Books, 1967. This is the ninth volume in the Conan series, which will run to at least twelve volumes when completed. As this is the only novel about Conan that Howard wrote, it is the best example of the Tolkienian elements in pure

Sword and Sorcery fiction and well worth reading on its own.

————— and Carter, Lin. *King Kull,* edited by Glenn Lord, New York, Lancer Books, 1967. An earlier series of tales laid in a pre-Atlantean age, completed by the present writer. It shows the influences of Lord Dunsany and Clark Ashton Smith.

Irving, Washington. *The Alhambra,* New York, James B. Millar and Co., 1884. Stories about the Moorish king Boabdil can be found throughout, but especially on pp. 67–73.

Keary, A. and E. *The Heroes of Asgard (Tales from Scandinavian Mythology),* New York, The Macmillan Co., 1893.

Kendall, Carol. *The Gammage Cup,* New York, Harcourt, Brace and Co., 1959.

—————. *The Whisper of Glocken,* New York, Harcourt, Brace and World, Inc., 1965.

Kershaw, N. *Stories and Battles of the Far Past,* Cambridge University Press, 1921. For data on the *Tháttr Nornagest* saga, etc.

Kready, Laura F. *A Study of Fairy Tales,* Chicago, Houghton Mifflin Co., 1916.

Lang, Andrew, *Prince Prigio,* Boston, Little, Brown and Co., 1942.

—————. "Prince Riccardo," in *My Own Fairy Book,* New York, Hurst and Co., n. d., pp. 89–190.

Lewis, C. S. *The Letters of C. S. Lewis,* edited and with an introduction by W. H. Lewis, New York, Harcourt, Brace and World., Inc., 1966. Contains much anecdotal material on Tolkien and his relations with Lewis, Charles Williams, etc., and background information on the period of the writing of the trilogy.

Lobeira, Vasco. *Amadis of Gaul,* translated from the Spanish version of García Ordóñez de Montalvo into English by Robert Southey, three vols., London, John Russell Smith, 1872.

Lovecraft, H. P. *The Dream Quest of Unknown Kadath,* Buffalo, Shroud Publishers, 1955. A curious and poetic fantasy novel, the culmination of Lovecraft's Dunsanian period and very unlike the horror fiction for which he is best known.

—————. *Dreams and Fancies,* with an introduction by August Derleth, Sauk City, Arkham House, 1962. Contains some of the early Dunsanian short stories, such as "Celephais" and "The Doom That Came to Sarnath," mentioned in Chapter 13.

———— et al. *The Shuttered Room (and Other Pieces),* Sauk City, Arkham House, 1959. For information on the puns and in-jokes among members of the "Lovecraft Circle," see Lin Carter, "H. P. Lovecraft: The Books," pp. 215, 218–219, 238, and 246.

Macdonald, George. *The Visionary Novels of George Macdonald,* edited by Anne Fremantle with an introduction by W. H. Auden, New York, The Noonday Press, 1954. Contains the two fantastic dream-romances, *Lilith* and *Phantastes,* which are often mentioned as a possible influence on Professor Tolkien. He has emphatically denied any influence by Macdonald, and in the judgment of the present writer, a study of the text confirms his statement.

Morris, William. *The Wood Beyond the World,* Boston, The Roberts House, 1895.

————. *The Well at the World's End,* London, Longmans, Green and Co., two vols., 1896.

————. *The Water of the Wondrous Isles,* London, Longmans, Green and Co., 1897. These three romances to a very large extent laid the foundations of the heroic fantasy tradition, and deserve the attention of Tolkien fans.

————. *The Life and Death of Jason (A Metrical Romance),* New York, Dodd, Mead and Co., 1917.

Parker, M. P. *The Allegory of the Faerie Queene,* Oxford University Press, 1960.

Pliny. *Natural History,* translated by H. Rackham, ten vols., London, William Heinemann, Ltd., 1961. The material in the footnote to Chapter 10 is drawn from Pliny, Vol. II., pp. 513–523.

Pratt, Fletcher. "The Blue Star," in *Witches Three,* with an introduction by John Ciardi, New York, Twayne Publishers, Inc., 1952, pp. 223–423.

———— (under the pseudonym of "George U. Fletcher"). *The Well of the Unicorn,* New York, William Sloane Associates, Inc., 1948. The most brilliant example of the epic fantasy novel written between the time of E. R. Eddison and the first publication of *The Lord of the Rings.* Issued in paperback by Lancer Books in 1968.

Quintus (of Smyrna). *The Fall of Troy,* translated by Arthur S. Way, London, William Heinemann, Ltd., 1913. An English verse translation, with original text on facing pages, of the *Posthomerica* epic.

Rydberg, Viktor. *Teutonic Mythology (Gods and Goddesses of the Northland),* translated from the Swedish by Rasmus B. Anderson, three vols., London, The Norroena Society,

1907. Published as Volumes III, IV, and V in the Norroena Series of the Anglo-Saxon Classics.

Saul, George Brandon. *The Shadow of the Three Queens (A Handbook Introduction to Traditional Irish Literature and its Backgrounds)*, Harrisburg, The Stackpole Company, 1953. A source used in Chapter 16; see for information on the Irish mythological history and its original texts.

Saxo (called "Grammaticus"). *The Nine Books of the Danish History*, translated by Oliver Elton, with an introduction by Frederick York Powell, two vols., London, The Norroena Society, 1905. English version of the *Gesta Danorum*, published as Volumes I and II in the Norroena Series of the Anglo-Saxon Classics.

Spence, Lewis. *The Fairy Tradition in Britain*, London, Rider and Co., 1948. A source of some of the information on the Tuatha de Danann used in Chapter 16.

Spenser, Edmund. *The Faerie Queene (Disposed into Twelve Bookes Fashioning XII Morall Vertues)*, with an introduction by John Hayward, New York, The Heritage Press, 1953.

Sturluson, Snorri. *The Heimskringla (A History of the Norse Kings)*, translated from the Icelandic by Samuel Laing, revised and with notes by Rasmus B. Anderson, three vols., London, The Norroena Society, 1907. For the appearance of Gandalf and Frode in the saga of Halfdan the Black, see vol. I, pp. 6–9 and 16.

———. *The Prose Edda*, translated from the Icelandic and with an introduction by Arthur Gilchrist Brodeur, New York, The American-Scandinavian Foundation, 1929.

Tillyard, E. M. W. *The English Epic and Its Background*, New York, Oxford University Press, 1954. A source used for data in Chapters 10, 11, and passim. See especially pp. 29, 32, 72–78, 124, 219.

Wagner, Richard. *The Ring of the Niblung*, translated by Margaret Armour, New York, Garden City Publishing Co., 1939. English verse translations of the four libretti which comprise the *Ring* tetralogy.

Wilkins, Ernest Hatch. *A History of Italian Literature*, Cambridge, Mass., Harvard University Press, 1954. A major source used for the latter half of Chapter 12.

ABOUT LIN CARTER

Well, I love dogs, and books, and swords, and Oz, and Barsoom, and collecting Egyptian antiquities, and *art nouveau*, and Chinese cloisónne. And Sax Rohmer, and *Paradise Lost*, and *The Three Imposters*, and Talbot Mundy, and Ezra Pound. And huge old Victorian houses, and having books published (22 so far), and my wonderful wife Noël—not quite in that order, of course! I like exploring through old, cobwebbed corners of literature, piecing together fragments of neglected Sumerian epics, finding gorgeousness in the *Shah Namah*, forgotten jewels in the *Shi-King*, or prowling the dusty pages of *Per em hru* (the Egyptian "Book of the Dead") and, in short, discovering wonder in old, old books nobody else bothers to read anymore.

Here's a thing I found just the other day. It's probably one of the best opening paragraphs anyone has ever written, but few have ever noticed it and certainly couldn't tell you what it's from:

> In the southern country is a city called Maiden's Delight. There lived a king named Immortal-Power. He was familiar with all the works treating of the wise conduct of life. His feet were made dazzling by the tangle of rays of light from jewels in the diadems of mighty kings who knelt before him. He had reached the far shore of all the arts that embellish life. This king had three sons. Their names were Rich-Power, Fierce-Power, Endless-Power, and they were supreme blockheads."

That was written thirteen hundred years ago. It's the first paragraph of a Sanskrit classic called The Five Books, or *Panchatantra*. It is one of the reasons that keep me busy exploring—and which makes my explorations joyous.

Lin Carter
New York, 1969

The great masterpieces of fantasy by
J. R. R. TOLKIEN

The Hobbit

and

The Lord of the Rings

Part I—THE FELLOWSHIP OF THE RING

Part II—THE TWO TOWERS

Part III—THE RETURN OF THE KING

plus
The Tolkien Reader

Smith of Wootton Major and Farmer Giles of Ham

The Road Goes Ever On: A Song Cycle
(music by Donald Swann)

Note: These are the complete and authorized paper-bound editions, published only by Ballantine Books.

To order by mail, send $1.00 for each book (except for *The Road Goes Ever On* which requires $3.00) to Dept. CS, Ballantine Books, 101 Fifth Avenue, New York, N. Y. 10003.

In Wildness Is the Preservation of the World

SELECTIONS & PHOTOGRAPHS BY
ELIOT PORTER

For many years the Sierra Club Exhibit books, priced at $25.00, have been recognized as examples of the finest bookmaking produced in America. Now, through the cooperation of the Sierra Club, and using the same presses and color separations used to produce the original edition, Ballantine Books is able to offer a selected number of these beautiful Exhibit books in a large-format (measuring 6½ by 9½) paperbound edition priced at $3.95.

The first title, *In Wildness Is the Preservation of the World,* is a 160-page book and contains all of the 72 page full-color plates. The photographs are by Eliot Porter, who also selected the accompanying text from the writings of Henry David Thoreau. The Introduction is by Joseph Wood Krutch.